Seasons on Whidbey

A sampler of
recipes celebrating
Fall, Winter,
Spring and Summer
on Whidbey Island,
Washington

Laura Moore
Deborah Skinner

Artwork by
Patti Gulledge White

SARATOGA  PUBLISHERS

SEASONS ON WHIDBEY

Additional copies may be purchased for retail price
plus $2.50 postage and handling per book.
For Washington delivery please include 7.9% sales tax.

Saratoga Publishers
1581 West Links Way
Oak Harbor, Washington 98277

Library of Congress Catalog No. 95-68281

ISBN 0-9628766-1-5

Printed in the United States of America.

First Printing August 1995

Seasons on Whidbey
is dedicated to a partnership based on friendship.
In our lives we have shared joy and laughter,
frustration and tears, failure and success.

Through the seasons our shared friendship has
provided support, rejoicing and great adventures.

... and to our husbands and children –
we are thankful for your patience
during production and
enthusiasm upon success.

• •

*"The language of
friendship is not
words, but
meanings.
It is an
intelligence
above language."*

Thoreau

• •

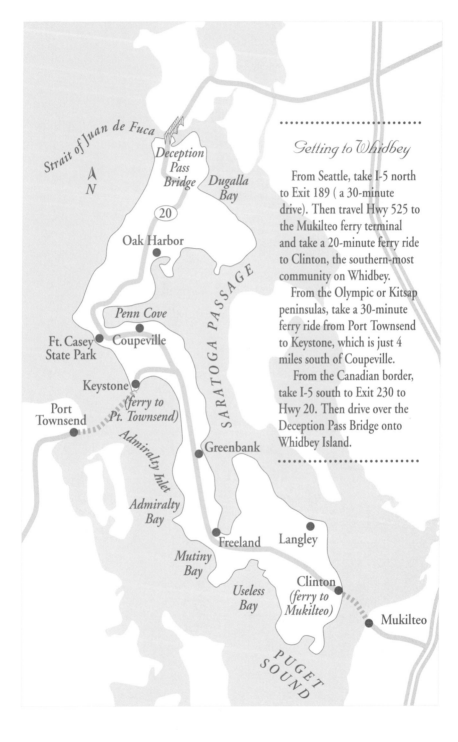

Strait of Juan de Fuca

Deception
Pass
Bridge

*Dugalla
Bay*

N

20

Oak Harbor

S A R A T O G A   P A S S A G E

Penn Cove

Ft. Casey
State Park

Coupeville

Keystone
*(ferry to
Pt. Townsend)*

Port
Townsend

Admiralty Inlet

Greenbank

*Admiralty
Bay*

Freeland

Langley

*Mutiny
Bay*

*Useless
Bay*

Clinton
*(ferry to
Mukilteo)*

Mukilteo

P U G E T
S O U N D

Getting to Whidbey

From Seattle, take I-5 north
to Exit 189 (a 30-minute
drive). Then travel Hwy 525 to
the Mukilteo ferry terminal
and take a 20-minute ferry ride
to Clinton, the southern-most
community on Whidbey.

From the Olympic or Kitsap
peninsulas, take a 30-minute
ferry ride from Port Townsend
to Keystone, which is just 4
miles south of Coupeville.

From the Canadian border,
take I-5 south to Exit 230 to
Hwy 20. Then drive over the
Deception Pass Bridge onto
Whidbey Island.

Admiralty Head Lighthouse
Cover Illustration

....

The Admiralty Head Lighthouse overlooks Admiralty Inlet and the Strait of Juan de Fuca. Originally constructed in 1860, the lighthouse was built as a signal for ships navigating the waters between Whidbey Island and the Olympic Peninsula. Considered out of date, the lighthouse was closed in 1927 and remained closed until Fort Casey became a park. Today, it is used as an interpretive center highlighting the history of Fort Casey. The lighthouse is full of historical displays and environmental exhibits including recent studies on beach monitoring, intertidal life, and a working model of Northern Puget Sound. Visitors are welcomed by volunteers who conduct tours of the lighthouse and park. Visitors can also enjoy a spectacular view of Admiralty Inlet from the top of the tower.

Whidbey Island is an island for all seasons.

September heralds the arrival of fall. The air is damp and chill, the shadows have shifted, the smell of burning leaves fills the air, and the days are noticeably shorter. Fog shrouded mornings bring cravings for earthy, warm meals that satisfy seasonal longings for foods like baked apples and roasted vegetables.

The pulse of nature slows during mild Whidbey winters. Holiday festivities, cozy fires, and friends and family warm spirits. It's a time to consider leisurely pursuits like reading, writing, and exploring island hiking trails. This is a time to ponder old dreams and new interests.

Spring brings renewal. Fish from the beach at Possession Park or from a boat on glacier formed Lake Pondilla. Watch for whales on the east side of Whidbey or kayak through Penn Cove and check out the activity at the mussel farm.

Warm summer days offer opportunities for beach walks, boating and barbecues. The long, mild days salute Langley's Choochokum, the Coupeville Arts and Crafts Festival, and picnics at Deception Pass State Park. Heady scents of wild flowers and warm salty air lull us through lazy afternoons.

Our yearnings for food change with the seasons. We hope you'll enjoy our suggestions for celebrating the "Seasons On Whidbey."

Table of Contents

~~~~~~~~~~~~~~~~~~~~~~~~~~~~

~~~~~~~~~~~~~~~~~~~~~~~~~~~~

*"We do not have to choose our
favorite among the seasons.
They are like our love for our
children. There's always
room for the next one.
It is only necessary for us
to see, and to rejoice in, the
beauty of their differences."*

Evelyn H. Lauder

"*Tomorrow's Pies*"

The Maxwelton apple orchard was planted in 1880 at the site of a thriving logging camp on South Whidbey. The fruit trees, bearing the "King of Tompkins County" apples, originated from upstate New York. They were planted for the residents of the camp, the Chinese cooks and the loggers. The pail in the picture was used to haul water from the creek to the old cabin where the cook worked long hours to provide meals for the men. The men worked all day to cut enormous trees with cross-cut saws. They often used an ox-drawn railway system to haul the logs to the Maxwelton mill, but occasionally the logs were simply skidded down the steep bluff and into the bay.

. . . .

"*When on the ground red apples lie*

In piles like jewels shining..."

And redder still on old stone walls

Are leaves of woodbine twining."

Helen Hunt Jackson
"October's Bright Blue Weather"

. . . .

List of Recipes ~ Fall

Maple Baked Apples

Saratoga Granola

Breakfast Apple Cobbler

Brie, Brie, and more Brie!

Marinated Shrimp and Artichoke Hearts

White Chicken Chili

Chef Rick's Cornbread

Coupe's Croutons

Dilled Coleslaw and other Fall Salads

Blue Cheese Bread

Nikita Salad

Pork Cutlets with Mushrooms and Sun Dried Tomato Sauce

Pommes au Gratin

Venison in Barbeque Sauce

Parsley Garlic Mashed Potatoes

Santa Fe Cafe Style Penn Cove Mussels

Autumn Pasta

Salmon Filet, Shrimp and Brie in Phyllo Crust

Hunter's Carrots

Chicken Breasts with Apple Cider Cream

Coconut Pudding with Caramel Sauce

German Chocolate Bars

Canoe Cookies

Granola Date Bars

Host a Chili Cook-Off party and invite your friends to bring their favorite version of this popular southwestern dish. Decorate your table with a large Jack-O-Lantern and straw flowers in old pottery. Encourage your guests to sample the wide variety of chili dishes.

Marinated Shrimp and Artichoke Hearts

Brie, Brie and more Brie! with Crackers

White Chicken Chili

Chef Rick's Cornbread

Nikita Salad

Cold Microbrews

German Chocolate Bars

Maple Baked Apples

When we think about our favorite foods or a food that makes us feel good, we usually remember one from our childhood like baked apples. These apples are plump and full of sweet tidbits that will melt in your mouth right away.

4 medium, firm apples
1/2 cup raisins or currants
2 tablespoons chopped walnuts
4 tablespoons brown sugar
1/2 cup, each, maple syrup and
   orange juice
1 teaspoon cinnamon
1 tablespoon sugar

Preheat oven to 350°. Core apples from the top and place in a shallow baking dish. Combine the raisins, walnuts and brown sugar and pack them into apple cavities. Pour the syrup and orange juice mixture evenly over the apples. Sprinkle the cinnamon and sugar over their tops. Bake for 45 minutes or until tender.

*"September
strews the
woodland o'er
With many a
brilliant color;
The world is
brighter than
before..."*

Thomas Wm. Parsons
from
"A Song For September"

Saratoga Granola

Some days just don't go well. You spill your first cup of coffee, the alarm wasn't set, you're late for an appointment... We all have days like this. You can give yourself an extra advantage when you begin your day with a bowl of Saratoga Granola.

In a saucepan, mix together:

1/2 teaspoon nutmeg
1/2 teaspoon cinnamon
1 teaspoon salt
1 teaspoon almond extract
1 tablespoon vanilla
1/2 cup honey
1/2 cup maple syrup
1/4 cup margarine, melted
1/2 cup vegetable oil

In a large bowl, combine:

1 1/2 cups bran flakes
2 cups rye flakes
1/2 cup wheat germ
3/4 cup oat bran
4 cups oats
1 cup coconut
3/4 cup slivered almonds
1/2 cup chopped walnuts
1/2 cup chopped cashews
3/4 cup pecans
3/4 cup macadamia nuts
1 cup raisins or currants
1/2 cup dried cranberries
    or cherries

Preheat oven to 300°. Spread the cereal mixture evenly on two cookie sheets. Drizzle the honey mixture over the cereal and toss gently to coat. Bake 30 minutes, mixing every 10 minutes. Cool completely and store in a tightly sealed container. This granola freezes well and is especially good when topped with fresh fruit and/or yogurt.

Breakfast Apple Cobbler

Warm cobbler gives a lazy weekend morning a certain grandeur.

1/3 cup packed brown sugar
2 tablespoons quick-cooking tapioca
1 1/2 teaspoons cinnamon
1 tablespoon lemon juice
4 large apples; peeled, cored, and sliced
1/3 cup raisins
1/3 cup butter
3/4 cup flour
1/3 cup oats
3 tablespoons sugar

Preheat oven to 375°. In a 2 quart casserole dish, mix brown sugar, tapioca, and cinnamon. Add lemon juice and 1/4 cup water; stir to mix. Let stand 20 minutes, stirring occasionally. Mix in apples and raisins. Bake for 15 minutes. Make crunchy topping by mixing butter, flour, oats, and sugar together. Remove cobbler from oven and stir well; crumble oat topping onto fruit. Place cobbler back into the oven and cook for 35 additional minutes. Spoon into bowls.

Sightings of American Bald Eagles are a common occurrence on Whidbey Island. Their numbers have substantially increased over the past few years. Their huge nests can be spotted in the high branches of the Douglas Fir and cedar trees. Watch for them all year long as they gracefully soar and circle above the island.

Brie, Brie and more Brie!

We're convinced that one of the best things to keep on hand is a wheel of Brie. Brie is a soft cheese (meaning fewer calories!) from France that can be enhanced in endless ways. We have several suggestions for serving Brie as an appealing appetizer or a simple dessert. Serve these at room temperature or bake the Brie in a 350° oven for 25-35 minutes.

- Slice Brie, horizontally, creating two layers. Spread pesto, snipped parsley and slivered almonds on top of one half. Sandwich the 2 layers of Brie together.

- Spoon chutney over the top of Brie.

- Drizzle honey or brown sugar on top of Brie; add chopped pecans.

- Thaw 1 sheet of frozen puff pastry according to directions. On a floured surface, roll out to a large circle, and place the round of Brie in the center of the pastry. Pull up the sides to enclose Brie, making sure that edges are sealed. Place seam side down on ungreased pan. Brush the top with 1 egg beaten with 1 teaspoon cream. Bake as directed above. This recipe can be prepared and frozen before washing the top and baking.

- Brie can bring a romantic end to an elegant meal when served with fresh fruit and a well chilled glass of Late Harvest white wine.

Marinated Shrimp and Artichoke Hearts

A great appetizer to make the night before you are expecting friends at your house.

1 cup oil
1/2 cup vinegar
1/3 cup white wine
1 tablespoon snipped parsley
1 teaspoon sugar
1/2 teaspoon salt
1/2 teaspoon paprika
1/4 teaspoon pepper
1 clove garlic
2 pounds medium shrimp, cooked
2 (14 ounce) cans artichoke hearts, drained
1 small onion, sliced into rings

Combine dressing ingredients and mix well. Place shrimp, artichoke hearts, and onion in a well sealed container. Pour marinade over all. Cover and store in refrigerator overnight, stirring occasionally. Drain and serve.

White Chicken Chili

Fall is the ideal season for a "chili cook-off."
We made large, orange wrapped invitations and
hand delivered them to our friends. We asked them
to bring their best chili and their most creative
Jack-O-Lantern to the "cook off." At the party we
enjoyed black bean chili, chili with cocoa, apples
and nuts, disguised Dinty Moore chili, chili with
tequila, and beanless chili, to name a few! We
tasted them all and voted for our favorite using
orange candycorns as our ballots. Nancy Wezeman
won 1st place at our cook-off with the following
tasty concoction.

2 pounds small white beans
6 boneless, skinned chicken breasts, diced
1/2 cup flour
1 (14 1/2 ounce) can vegetable broth
1 (14 1/2 ounce) can chicken broth
1 (2 1/2 ounce) can sliced olives
1 (4 ounce) can diced green chilies
1 teaspoon chili powder
salt and pepper to taste
1 tablespoon diced onions
1 pint half and half
1 cup sour cream

Cover white beans with water and soak overnight.
Rinse, replace in pan, cover with water, and cook
over low heat for 1 1/2 hours. Sauté chicken in 1
tablespoon butter. Sprinkle with flour to thicken
the broth that forms. Add chicken to beans along
with broth, olives, chilies and their juices. Add
spices and onions. Continue to simmer until beans
are soft. When beans are cooked, add the half and
half and sour cream; heat throughout.

*For dessert,
Liz Kline created
a terrific
pumpkin cake by
making two cakes
in bundt pans;
putting them
together to form a
pumpkin shape.
She frosted it
bright orange
and used candy
for the face.
It made a great
table centerpiece!*

Chef Rick's Cornbread

We've always believed Rick Chapman is a great chef. In fact, the cornbread that he brought to our chili cook-off was fantastic. However, we couldn't believe it when he confessed that he had just added a couple ingredients to the old standby, "Jiffy Cornbread Mix!"

1 (8 1/2 ounce) pkg. cornbread mix		1 pkg. cornbread mix
1/4 cup honey	or	1 (4 ounce) can chilies
2 tablespoons Jack cheese		1/4 cup cheddar cheese

Combine the three ingredients along with those on the boxed package. Cook in an 8 inch pan according to package directions.

Coupe's Croutons

Make a batch of these to toss on the green salad you'll serve with the chili!

4 slices French, Italian, or Sourdough bread
1/4 cup olive oil
1/2 tablespoon minced parsley
dash of oregano
2 cloves minced garlic
1/4 cup grated Parmesan cheese

Cut bread slices into 1/2 inch cubes. Sauté cubes in olive oil, over medium heat, for 3 minutes. Toss often. Add parsley, oregano and garlic. Sauté for 1 minute longer, or until bread is brown and crisp. Remove from heat and sprinkle with Parmesan. Toss well.

Brighten a midweek supper with any one of these ideas for simple, healthy salad-vegetable duos.

Dilled Coleslaw

....

1/2 head green cabbage	2 tablespoons lemon juice
1/2 head red cabbage	2 tablespoons sugar
1 cup mayonnaise	1 tablespoon fresh dill
1 cup light sour cream	or 1 teaspoon dried dill
1/2 teaspoon capers	

Shred cabbage and place in a large salad bowl. Combine dressing ingredients and mix well. Pour dressing over cabbage and season.

Green Bean Salad

....

Rinse fresh green beans and cut the end tips off. Blanch the beans for 3 - 5 minutes. Drain and allow to cool. Cut several fresh tomatoes into bite size pieces. Put the beans and tomatoes in a large bowl and toss with your favorite Italian dressing. Add bits of Mozzarella cheese. Chill and serve!

Greek Salad

....

This salad can be prepared in the dish in which you will serve it. Peel and slice 2 cucumbers and place them in the dish. Layer sliced tomatoes, onions and black olives over the cucumbers. Crumble Feta cheese and drizzle extra virgin olive oil over the vegetables. Cut a lemon in half across the center and squeeze the juice from both halves overall. Serve at room temperature.

Red Pepper Tortellini Salad

....

Cook tortellini, drain and rinse with cold water. Drain again. In a large bowl, mix Catalina dressing with tortellini, to taste. Using a jar of roasted peppers in oil, add large chopped pieces to tortellini. Sprinkle chopped green onion on top. Cover and chill.

Blue Cheese Bread

Pungent Blue cheese provides a surprising flavor in this bread.

2 ounces yeast
4 tablespoons sugar
7 - 8 cups flour
1 cup milk
1 tablespoon salt
3 tablespoons butter
2 tablespoons dehydrated onion
2 eggs
1 teaspoon Worcestershire sauce
2 ounces Blue cheese
1 tablespoon chopped chives

"The best smell is bread, the best saver salt, the best love that of children."

George Herbert

Dissolve yeast in 1 1/2 cups lukewarm water. Stir in 2 tablespoons sugar and 1 1/2 cups flour until smooth. Allow mixture to sit for 20 minutes or until it bubbles. Combine 2 tablespoons sugar, salt, butter and onions. Scald milk and pour over the sugar mixture. When the sugar mixture is luke-warm, add it to the yeast mixture. Add 2 eggs and Worcestershire sauce. Stir in 5 - 6 cups flour, Blue cheese and chives. Empty dough onto 1 cup flour and knead until smooth. Put dough in a greased bowl and invert to oil the top. Cover with plastic wrap and let the dough rise for 1 hour. After dough has risen, punch down and form 3 loaves. Place in 3 loaf pans. Allow to rise for 45 minutes, covered with a damp cloth. Preheat oven to 350°. Score tops. Brush with milk and bake for 35 -45 minutes.

Nikita Salad

Chutney is a surprise ingredient in this colorful and tasty salad. You can avoid a pre-dinner snack attack by serving a salad while you prepare the rest of the meal! Keep a supply of clean, dry salad greens on hand. Rinsed greens, wrapped in towels to drain, will stay fresh if they are enclosed in a plastic bag and well chilled.

1 head romaine
1 bunch spinach
2 red Delicious apples, cored and diced
1/2 cup chopped walnuts
1/2 cup chopped green onion

Chutney Dressing

1/4 cup olive oil
1 tablespoon rice vinegar
1/2 teaspoon lemon juice
1 tablespoon mango chutney
1/4 teaspoon curry

Tear greens into bite size pieces. Place in a bowl with apples and walnuts. Combine dressing ingredients and shake well. Pour dressing over salad just before serving.

Pork Cutlets with Mushrooms and Sun Dried Tomato Sauce

Pork cutlets constitute a perfect autumn meal. The sun dried tomatoes add color to the mushroom sauce and a distinctive flavor as well. Serve the cutlets with rice pilaf and a steamed vegetable.

oil for browning
8 pork cutlets, trimmed of fat and pounded
1 pound fresh mushrooms, sliced
1/4 cup chopped green onion
2 cloves minced garlic
1 (14 1/2 ounce) can chicken broth
4 tablespoons Dijon mustard
1/2 cup chopped sun dried tomatoes
1 teaspoon grated orange peel

Heat oil in a large skillet. Cook pounded cutlets for 4 - 5 minutes on each side, or until no longer pink. Remove cutlets to a platter and keep warm. Add 1 teaspoon oil, mushrooms, onion and garlic to the drippings in the skillet. Cook for 3 minutes; stirring until light brown. Add chicken broth and bring to a boil; stirring constantly. Add mustard, tomatoes and orange peel. Cook for an additional 3 minutes. Spoon sauce over warm cutlets.

Pommes au Gratin

A favorite for any season!

1 clove garlic
1 tablespoon butter
2 pounds potatoes, peeled and thinly sliced
1 1/2 teaspoons salt
1/2 teaspoon pepper
3 cups half and half, scalded and cooled
1/8 teaspoon nutmeg
1 cup grated Gruyere or Swiss cheese

Preheat oven to 350°. Slice the garlic clove in half. Rub a casserole dish with the garlic pieces and then with the butter. Arrange the potato slices in the dish and sprinkle with the seasonings. In a small bowl, beat the egg with the half and half. Pour over potatoes. Sprinkle cheese on top. Bake for 1 hour.

Venison in Barbecue Sauce

Gail Neil often has the results of her husband's hunting trips stocked in her freezer. When Gail prepares venison, she allows it to cook slowly in a crock pot or a Dutch oven. This tenderizes the meat and lets it absorb the flavors of the barbecue sauce.

1/3 cup Worcestershire sauce
1/8 teaspoon chili powder
1 teaspoon salt
dash Tabasco
1 cup ketchup
2 cloves minced garlic
2 pounds venison

Mix all ingredients, except venison and garlic, in a large saucepan with 2 cups water. Cook over medium heat, stirring constantly. Allow the sauce to come to a boil. Brown the venison in a Dutch oven. Remove it from the pan and add garlic to the drippings. Cook, scraping drippings for 4 minutes. Return the meat to the pot, pour the sauce over the meat and cover. Allow the meat to simmer over medium low heat for 3-4 hours.

Whidbey Island was formed by glaciers in the last Ice Age. The area surrounding Ft. Ebey State Park shows evidence of the Vashon Glacier. As this glacier retreated, it left behind chunks of ice that were buried by rocks and debris. When the ice melted, steep depressions or "kettleholes," were left in the ground. People who explore the hiking trails at Ebey State Park will find that their path takes them in and out of these wooded kettleholes.

*Bundle up and take a walk on the
beach in the autumn fog and drizzle.
Come home to a hearty meal that you
can relish in front of a roaring fire.*

Rhubarb Wine from Whidbey Island Winery

Pork Cutlets with Mushrooms and
Sun Dried Tomato Sauce

Pommes au Gratin

Hunter's Carrots

Green Bean Salad

Coconut Pudding with Caramel Sauce

Parsley Garlic Mashed Potatoes

The ingredients and preparation are simple...but the taste is divine!

5 medium potatoes, peeled
1 bulb garlic, unpeeled and roasted
4 tablespoons butter
1/3 cup milk
3 tablespoons snipped parsley
salt and pepper to taste

Boil potatoes in 4 cups salted water until tender. Drain and transfer to a large bowl. Squeeze garlic into bowl and mash the potatoes. Stir in butter, milk, parsley and season.

Santa Fe Cafe Style Penn Cove Mussels

Whidbey Island's Penn Cove is a quiet, pristine place that has become one of the most famous mussel farming areas in the world. The mussels, produced by Penn Cove Mussels. Inc., are grown on ropes suspended beneath rafts that are anchored in the cool waters of the cove. This spicy recipe is quick and easy to prepare and is sure to bring accolades from your guests!

2 1/2 cups, plus 1/4 cup olive oil
1/2 red onion, diced
1/2 yellow bell pepper, diced
2 tablespoons minced garlic
2 tablespoons green scallions, chopped
1/4 cup hot green chilies
1/2 cup fresh lime juice
2 large tomatoes, diced
1 red bell pepper, diced
3 tablespoons cilantro, chopped
1 tablespoon red chili flakes
1 teaspoon, each, salt and pepper
5 pounds Penn Cove Mussels
3/4 cup white wine

Prepare marinade 4 hours in advance: whisk together the lime juice and 2 1/2 cups olive oil. Stir in all other ingredients except the mussels, remaining oil and wine. Cover and let stand at room temperature.

Remove any remaining beards from the mussels and rinse the mussels under fresh water. Steam the mussels in the remaining olive oil and white wine until all shells are open. Discard any mussels that do not open during cooking. Spoon mussels, in their shells, into serving bowls and pour marinade over mussels. Serve immediately.

Entrees for 5
Appetizers for 10 - 20

Autumn Pasta

Don't miss the opportunity to stop by roadside produce stands to enjoy the brilliant colors of big, full baskets overflowing with late summer fruits and vegetables. Autumn Pasta is a healthy, satisfying dish without meat, fish or poultry. Serve the pasta with a green salad and crusty Blue Cheese Bread. The roasted vegetables will also be excellent when served with a grilled red meat.

2 red onions
3 peppers; red, yellow, green or orange
1 small eggplant
2 zucchini
1 crooked neck, yellow squash
salt and pepper to taste
1/4 cup olive oil
1 tablespoon Balsamic vinegar
2 teaspoons "fines herbes" (1/2 teaspoon,
    each, parsley, chervil, chives and tarragon)
5 cloves garlic, peeled and crushed
12 ounces pasta (such as linguini)
4 tablespoons Parmesan cheese
1/4 teaspoon red pepper flakes
2 teaspoons chopped parsley

Preheat oven to 425°. Thickly slice or cube vegetables to uniform size and spread on a large baking sheet. Season with salt and pepper. Bake for 30 minutes. Change oven setting to broil, and brown vegetables under the broiler for 2 - 3 minutes. In a small bowl, combine oil, vinegar, herbs and garlic. When vegetables are finished cooking, return to large bowl and cover with dressing. Cook pasta according to package directions; drain. Add cooked pasta to the bowl of vegetables. Season with Parmesan, pepper flakes and parsley.

Three miles south of Deception Pass lies Duqualla Bay Farm, "The Oasis of Whidbey." The rustic old barn is brimming with fresh local and organic produce during the summer and fall months. They make their own jams and jellies from the vast assortment of berries grown in the flats of Duqualla Bay. You can pick your own berries and pumpkins or let the staff do it for you! Inside the barn there are big bouquets of fresh wild flowers in buckets and dried flowers and herbs hanging from the wooded beams above. You will always receive a warm welcome from the owners, the Hulbert's, and their hard working staff.

Salmon Filet, Shrimp and Brie in a Phyllo Crust

Scott Fraser, chef at Kasteel Franssen in Oak Harbor, was trained in the traditional French cooking school, Pierre Dubrulle, in Vancouver, British Columbia. Scott has incorporated his skills in French cooking with further training he received from several restaurants emphasizing the preparation of Northwest cuisine. The result, a presentation of fresh foods enhanced by flavorful herbs and sauces that allow "heart healthy" gourmet dining.

4 six-ounce salmon filets	12 pieces Phyllo sheets
6 ounces cooked bay shrimp	olive oil
4 ounces Brie cheese	salt and pepper to taste

Preheat oven to 400°. Season salmon filets with salt and pepper. Place one ounce of Brie on each salmon. Divide shrimp between the salmon and place on top of the Brie. With a pastry brush, lightly coat one Phyllo sheet with olive oil and place the second sheet on top. Lightly coat the second sheet with oil and place third sheet on top. Brush oil around edge of third sheet. Place salmon in the middle. Fold the Phyllo around the salmon. Repeat for all salmon pieces. Bake for 20-25 minutes until salmon is cooked through. Finish the presentation with Whidbey's Loganberry Sauce.

Whidbey's Loganberry Sauce

6 ounces honey	1/2 cup *Whidbey's* liqueur
1 cup white wine vinegar	3/4 unsalted butter, cubed
1 cup fresh or frozen loganberries	

In a heavy saucepan, bring the honey to a boil. Reduce until it becomes a hazelnut color. Add vinegar and the berries. Reduce by one-third. Add liqueur and reduce until 1 cup liquid remains. Over medium heat, whisk in cold butter cubes, a little at a time, until incorporated. Keep warm until drizzling over the salmon.

Hunter's Carrots

Simply appealing!

5 cups carrots, julienned
2 tablespoons butter
1 teaspoon salt
1/4 teaspoon cinnamon
1 teaspoon grated orange peel
2 tablespoons honey
2 teaspoons lemon juice

Cover carrots with water in a skillet
and add butter and salt. Cover and
cook just until tender. Add more water,
if necessary to prevent sticking.
When carrots are tender and liquid is
almost gone, stir in cinnamon, orange
peel, honey and lemon juice.
Simmer for 3 minutes and serve.

*"From gold
to gray
Our mild
sweet day
Of Indian summer
fades too soon;
But tenderly
Above the sea
Hang's white
and calm,
the hunter's
moon."*

John Greenleaf Whittier
from
"Indian Summer"

Chicken Breasts with Apple Cider Cream

If you are in a hurry, but would like to fix a tasty main dish, try browning chicken breasts as described at right. Before serving, sprinkle the chicken with "Mutiny Bay Gourmet" loganberry vinegar. Creators, Marcia Comer and Karen Erskine, use fresh picked loganberries from Greenbank to blend with rice vinegar and white wine vinegar. They assure us the vinegar is "berry good" when used on chicken and pork.

A perfect main dish for a fall meal.

4 chicken breasts, skinned, boned and halved
1/2 cup butter
1/2 teaspoon, each, salt and pepper
1 medium onion, chopped
1 tablespoon parsley
1/4 teaspoon thyme
1/4 teaspoon rosemary
3/4 cup apple cider
1 cup light cream
1 tablespoon cornstarch

Melt the butter in a large sauté pan. Season the chicken with salt and pepper and arrange in the pan. Over medium heat, brown the chicken until golden brown on both sides, about 15 minutes. Add the onion, seasonings, and cider to the pan. Cover and simmer for 15 minutes. Remove chicken from the pan and keep warm in the oven. Add cream to the pan and slowly sprinkle cornstarch to the mixture. Use a small whip to incorporate. Cook until the sauce thickens, remove from pan. Place the chicken on a serving dish and pour the cider cream over the chicken.

Coconut Pudding with Caramel Sauce

This pudding is a proven palate pleaser! Use fresh coconut if it is available and your time allows for the extra effort needed for preparation.

2 cups half and half
2 tablespoons unflavored gelatin
1 cup sugar
1 teaspoon almond extract
2 cups grated coconut, fresh or packaged
3 cups heavy cream, whipped

Place cream in a saucepan and bring to a boil. Soak gelatin in a little cold water and add sugar. When sugar and gelatin have dissolved, add to the cream and cool. When cooled, add almond extract and coconut. Fold whipped cream into the mixture. Pour the pudding into a mold and refrigerate for 6 hours or until it is firm. To serve, remove pudding from mold, sprinkle with coconut and spoon caramel sauce over individual servings.

" A good cook is like a sorceress who dispenses happiness."

Elsa Schiaparelli

Caramel Sauce

1 tablespoon butter
2 1/2 cups brown sugar
2 egg yolks
1 cup cream
1/8 teaspoon salt
1 teaspoon vanilla

Combine all ingredients except vanilla. Cook in a double boiler pan until sauce is smooth. Remove from heat, cool, and add vanilla.

German Chocolate Bars

Everyone needs a recipe like this. Whether the bars are served at a meeting of great minds (and eager appetites), or placed in the midst of starving teenagers, Freida Weaver guarantees these chocolate treats will be popular.

1 (4 ounce) German Chocolate bar
5 tablespoons butter
3 ounces cream cheese
1 cup sugar
3 eggs
1/2 cup and 1 tablespoon flour
2 teaspoons vanilla
1/4 teaspoon almond extract

Preheat oven to 350° and grease a 9x13 inch pan. In a small bowl, melt the chocolate with 2 table-spoons of the butter. Set aside. In another bowl blend the cream cheese with 1/4 cup of the sugar. Add 1 egg, 1 tablespoon flour and 1 teaspoon of the vanilla. Set aside. In a separate bowl beat 2 eggs. Add 3/4 cup sugar, the baking powder and 1/2 cup flour. Mix well. Blend the chocolate mixture into this. Add 1 teaspoon vanilla and the almond extract. If desired, add nuts. Spread half of the chocolate batter into the pan. Top with the cream cheese mixture, covering as much of the batter as possible. Top with the rest of the batter. Bake for 30 minutes. Sprinkle with powdered sugar and cut into bars before the cake cools.

Canoe Cookies

These versatile pastries can be used as a dessert or an hors d'oeuvre simply by changing the sweet filling to a favorite meat, seafood or cheese mixture.

1/2 cup butter	1/2 cup sugar
1/2 cup cottage cheese	1 /2 teaspoon cinnamon
1 teaspoon vanilla	1/2 cup chopped walnuts
1 cup flour	1 egg, separated

In a mixing bowl, cream the butter; add the cottage cheese and vanilla. Gradually add flour until a ball is formed. Chill for 30 minutes. Preheat oven to 375°. Combine sugar, cinnamon and nuts in a small bowl. Roll dough to 1/8 inch thickness and cut into 4 inch squares. Spoon 1 teaspoon filling in the center of each square. Begin at one corner of each square and fold into an envelope shape. Beat egg yolk with 1 teaspoon water. Brush over each cookie. Sprinkle with sugar and bake for 20 minutes.

Granola Date Bars

These bars are great for a mid-day coffee break. They are particularly tasty when you use Saratoga Granola, one of our recipes included in this book!

1 egg	1/3 cup raisins
1/3 cup brown sugar	1/4 cup chopped pecans
1/2 teaspoon vanilla	1 1/3 cups granola
1/2 cup chopped dates	

Preheat oven to 350°. In a medium size bowl, mix egg, sugar and vanilla together. Add dates, raisins, pecans and granola. Mix well. Press into a greased 8 inch pan. Bake for 25 minutes. Cool before cutting.

～ Winter ～

"Dusk at Silliman Cabin, Maxwelton Bluff"

The Silliman cabin was built before World War I on the site of a logging camp on Whidbey's south end. It was used as a cookhouse by the Chinese cooks who worked there. The rustic old cabin has been owned by the Silliman family for several generations. They have used the cabin for their summer recreation, and it has been preserved to look as it did in the early 1900's. There has never been electricity to the old cabin.

· ·

"Winter, still I see

Many charms in thee,

Love thy chilly greeting,

Snow-storms fiercely beating..."

from "Winter Song" by Ludwig Holty

· ·

Gulledge-White

List of Recipes ~ Winter

Fort Casey Muesli
Maxwelton Manor Dutch Babies
Whidbey English Muffins
Senegalese Soup
Country Crackers
Holiday Herb Spread
Roasted Red Pepper Dip
Roasted Garlic
Mustard Tarragon Beef
Broccoli Gorgonzola Salad
Stuffed Onions
Greek Prawns
Wild Rice Pilaf
Oven Roasted Chicken with Rosemary and White Wine
Winter Salad with Buttermilk Dressing
Vegetable Medley
Stockpot Seafood
Leeks in Red Wine
Pinot Noir Truffles
Irish Coffee
Praline Parfait
Bittersweet Fudge Sauce
Chocolate Currant Torte
White Chocolate Macadamia Nut Cookies
"For the Birds"

*Invite a few special friends to greet the holidays
with you. Set round tables with sparkling crystal
and lots of shimmering candles. Have your friends
help decorate your home for the holidays and, for
a nostalgic touch, give each guest a decoration to
take home with them.*

Senegalese Soup

Country Crackers with Roasted Garlic

Mustard Tarragon Beef

Wild Rice Pilaf

Leeks in Red Wine

Winter Salad

Pinot Noir Truffles

Whidbey's Port

Fort Casey Muesli

Originally, Fort Casey Inn was home to five officers who served in the U.S. Army. It was built before the First World War. Victoria and Gordon Hoenig purchased the homes as a restoration project. However, they soon developed a passion to create a bed & breakfast inn that would reflect the "generous spirit of caring" so prevalent during wartime. The Hoenig's relied upon a simple breakfast of Muesli before starting each day of renovation. Their project took 3 1/2 years to complete and encompassed over 50 rooms!

3 cups rolled oats
1 1/2 cups wheat germ
1/2 cup bran
1/4 cup soy flakes
1/4 cup ground hazelnuts
1/4 cup chopped walnuts
1/4 cup raisins
1/4 cup chopped dried apricots
1/4 cup dried cranberries

Combine all ingredients and place in a covered container. Store in a cool, dry place. At serving time, mix some of the dry ingredients with yogurt to make a creamy consistency. Or, prepare as you would a hot cereal. Top with fresh fruits or berries.

Fort Casey Inn is a row of island cottages that overlook Puget Sound. The owners have maintained the simplicity of the buildings and filled them with patriotic memorabilia. They have mixed military motifs, folk art, and feminine accessories masterfully throughout the homes. You'll find treasures such as a turn-of-the-century quilt, framed advertisements, a German bed with a drum as a nightstand, and old flags. They also have a 20th century cupboard stocked with hand embroidered First World War pillows and a bust of George Washington. The Inn is a perfect place for family reunions, weddings, or just a quiet retreat.

43 ❄

Maxwelton Manor Dutch Babies

Sonny and Nancy Richardson invite guests to take a step back in time with a visit to their colonial bed & breakfast inn. Nestled in the trees outside of Langley, the Manor is a reproduction of a home built in 1830. Six acres of woods and groomed paths surrounding the home have been certified as an official Backyard Wildlife Sanctuary by the State of Washington. Guests take particular delight in the friendly llamas that roam the property. Breakfast is always served by candlelight and on gray mornings a fire is set in the Rumford fireplace.

2 Washington apples, peeled and sliced
1/2 cup butter or margarine, plus 1 tablespoon
5 large eggs
1 1/4 cups milk
1 1/4 cups flour
cinnamon, ground nutmeg and
   powdered sugar to taste

Preheat oven to 425°. In a stove top pan cook the apple slices in 1 table-spoon butter over medium high heat. Sprinkle with cinnamon. Melt the 1/2 cup butter in the oven in a deep pan, such as a paella pan or pie plate. While the butter melts, quickly whirl eggs at high speed, gradually adding milk and flour. Mix for 30 seconds. Add the apple slices to the pan from the oven with the melted butter. Pour the batter over the apples. Return the pan to the oven and bake until pancake is puffy and the edges are browned, 20-25 minutes. Cut in wedges and dust with nutmeg and powdered sugar. Top with Apple Syrup, if desired.

Whidbey English Muffins

On a chilly winter weekend lure your family to the kitchen with the smell of baking bread wafting through your house.

1 package active dry yeast
1/2 cup scalded milk
2 teaspoons sugar
1 teaspoon salt
4 cups flour
3 tablespoons softened butter

Dissolve the yeast in 2 tablespoons warm water for 4 minutes.
Combine the milk, sugar, and salt with 1 cup water in a mixing bowl.
Add the yeast mixture to the bowl, stir well. In a large bowl, gradually mix the yeast mixture with 2 cups of the flour. Cover the bowl with a cloth and let the dough rise in a warm place for about 1 1/2 hours, or until it collapses back into the bowl. Beat in the butter, and then beat in the remaining 2 cups flour. Knead the bread on a floured surface for a few minutes.

Grease the inside of 6 English Muffin rings, if you have them, and fill them 1/2 full with the batter. Otherwise, grease a baking sheet and form muffin shapes about 2 inches tall and 4 inches in diameter. Let the muffins stand until the dough has doubled in bulk. Preheat oven to 425°. Bake the muffins until golden brown in color, about 15 minutes. Cool slightly. Smother with butter and jam.

Senegalese Soup

When Caryn Riley moved to Oak Harbor from the east coast she brought with her a wealth of knowledge about food and creative ways in which to prepare and serve it. Her kitchen is one of her favorite places whether she is working hard on a catering job or cooking for friends.

"While the pot boils, friendship blooms."

A.B. Cheales

1 cup butter
7 shallots, minced
3 celery stalks, chopped
1/2 cup flour
3/4 cup sherry
3/4 cup apple cider
3/4 cup chicken broth
4 cups milk
1 pound chicken breast, cooked and chopped
1 1/2 teaspoons curry powder
1/2 teaspoon dill weed
1 teaspoon pepper
chopped apple for garnish

In a large saucepan, sauté butter, shallots and celery. Whisk in flour and stir for 3 minutes. Slowly add sherry, cider and broth; stirring constantly. Gradually add milk. Stir and add chicken. Simmer for 20 minutes over medium heat. Blend in curry, dill and pepper. Simmer until serving time. Garnish each bowl of soup with chopped apple.

Country Crackers

Enjoy a light wafer with soup or tea on a chilly Whidbey winter afternoon. Cut the wafers into a special shape to fit the occasion!

2 cups whole wheat flour
1 teaspoon salt
1/2 teaspoon baking powder
1/4 cup margarine
1/2 cup milk
1 egg
coarse salt

Preheat oven to 400°. Sift flour, salt and baking powder together. Cut in the margarine until the flour is the consistency of cornmeal. Stir in milk and egg to form a stiff dough. Knead for 5 minutes or until the dough leaves the sides of the bowl. On a floured board, roll the dough until it is very thin. Cut the dough into squares, rounds or various shapes with cookie cutters. Place shapes on a greased cookie sheet and sprinkle with coarse salt, if desired. Prick each shape with a fork and bake for 10 minutes, or until lightly browned.

Holiday Herb Spread

Make unexpected guests welcome during the holiday season. Keep a loaf of this herb spread on hand to serve well wishers who drop by your home for a visit.

2 (8 ounce) packages cream cheese
1/4 pound unsalted butter
4 ounces sliced Proscuitto
2 cups snipped parsley
3 teaspoons grated lemon peel
1/2 cup chopped green onion

Allow the cream cheese and butter to soften to room temperature. Line a 3 x 5 inch loaf pan with the Proscuitto, reserving 1 slice. Using a food processor, whirl the cream cheese, butter, parsley, lemon peel and onion together until well blended. Spoon half the cheese mixture into the pan without disturbing the Proscuitto lining. Cover with another slice of Proscuitto. Top with remaining cheese mixture. Fold any meat that overlaps the cheese mixture onto the filling. Cover and chill overnight. Invert the pan onto a serving dish and serve with breadsticks or crackers.

Holiday Herb Spread can be tightly covered with plastic wrap and frozen. Bring to room temperature before serving.

Roasted Red Pepper Dip

Roasted red peppers have become very popular since they are often used in sauces for pastas and fish, and as garnish for a host of other foods. The vibrant color and scent of a roasted red pepper is particularly alluring. This dip is especially festive when placed in the center of a cored and seeded red pepper. Surround the pepper with fresh vegetables.

1 cup mayonnaise
1/2 cup plain yogurt
1/3 cup roasted red peppers in oil
1 teaspoon basil
1/4 teaspoon red pepper flakes

Process or blend all ingredients. Chill until serving.

On North Whidbey you'll find the Atelier Holly Farm, a family owned business that has operated for many, many years. As the holiday season approaches, the groves of full holly trees are harvested to create exquisite holly wreaths, swags and bouquets enjoyed by islanders and sent as Christmas greetings all over the world. Fill a basket with sprigs of holly and have it out when friends come to visit. Before they leave, let each guest throw a sprig into your fire to make a wish for good luck!

Roasted Garlic

Roasted garlic, cooked in its husk, loses its pungency and can be served like butter with toasted bread rounds, tart apple slices, baked Brie and a hearty glass of Cabernet. This is the perfect appetizer prior to a beef entreé.

**1 large clove garlic -
   preferably Elephant garlic
olive oil**

Slice off the top of the garlic bulb. Peel off the loose outer leaves without removing entire husk. Drizzle garlic head with olive oil and place in a garlic baker. Cover or wrap loosely in foil. Place the garlic in a cold oven. Set temperature for 300° and bake for 30 minutes. Remove cover and bake an additional 45 minutes; basting with olive oil occasionally. To serve, squeeze the garlic out of the cloves directly onto bread rounds.

Mustard Tarragon Beef

It is difficult to improve the mouth-watering flavor of a well grilled steak or a baked tenderloin. However, this sauce comes very close, especially when fresh tarragon is used. Try adding some of the juice from your beef for a fuller taste.

1 pound lean, boneless beef
2 tablespoons dry red wine
2 tablespoons Dijon mustard
1 teaspoon ground pepper
2 cloves minced garlic
1 cup mushrooms, sliced and sauteéd

Combine mustard, red wine, pepper and garlic. Coat beef on both sides with this mixture and place in a shallow dish. Cover and refrigerate 8 hours. Prepare sauce for beef. When ready to serve, grill or broil beef to desired degree of doneness. Let stand for 5 minutes. Thinly slice steak across the grain and transfer to a warm platter. Place sauteéd mushrooms on top of beef and spoon Mustard Tarragon Sauce over all.

Mustard Tarragon Sauce

3 tablespoons softened butter
2 tablespoons Dijon mustard
1/4 cup minced shallot
1 cup white wine
1 1/2 tablespoons minced fresh tarragon
1 tablespoon heavy cream

Cream the butter and mustard in a small dish. In a small saucepan combine the shallots, wine and tarragon. Cook over medium high heat until the wine is reduced to 3 tablespoons. Reduce heat and stir in cream. Whisk in mustard butter and season to taste.

Broccoli Gorgonzola Salad

Broccoli is an exceptional member of the cabbage family. It has more flavor than cauliflower and it is less pungent than cabbage. Broccoli is one of the most versatile vegetables since it lends itself to all cooking methods. It is also extremely popular served as a "crudité," which is a big bonus since raw broccoli is filled with calcium, vitamins A and C.

When serving, arrange broccoli spears on lettuce lined salad plates. Spoon the dressing evenly over each plate and garnish with sliced radishes.

1/2 pounds broccoli, steamed
4 tablespoons olive oil
3 tablespoons lemon juice
1/4 cup chopped green onion
1/4 teaspoon, each, salt, pepper and
  dry mustard
2 cloves minced garlic
1/2 cup crumbled Gorgonzola cheese
6 sliced radishes

Chill steamed broccoli for 4 - 6 hours. Combine oil, lemon juice, green onion, and seasonings in a small jar. Shake well. Add cheese and refrigerate until serving.

Stuffed Onions

An ordinary entreé can be enhanced
when you serve an unusual, but flavorful
accompaniment such as these stuffed
onions.

6 medium yellow onions
1/2 cup chopped ham
1/2 cup plus 2 tablespoons bread crumbs
1/2 teaspoon salt
1/4 teaspoon pepper
1 tablespoon margarine
1/2 cup milk

Preheat oven to 400°. Remove a 1 inch slice
from the top of each onion and place the
onion in boiling water. Parboil until almost
tender (about 10 minutes). Drain onions
and remove centers, leaving 6 small cups.
In a sauté pan, melt the margarine and
brown the ham, 1/2 cup bread crumbs and
the seasonings. Fill the onion cups with the
ham mixture. Place the cups in a baking
dish and sprinkle with remaining crumbs.
Pour the milk around the cups. Bake for
20 minutes.

*It is not true that
island residents
have webbed feet.
In fact, Whidbey
has a very
temperate climate
because it lies
in the
"rain shadow"
of the Olympic
mountains.
Central Whidbey,
which receives
about 18 inches
of rain per year,
has less than half
the amount of
rain as the
mainland does.*

Greek Prawns

Roger and Debra Simmons realized a dream when they were able to build "Teddy's," a large Victorian restaurant in Freeland. Welcomed with the warmth of a fire, you'll appreciate the lush deep booths, the tulip light fixtures and the mahogany wainscotting; enticing you to stay awhile. The bar is an attraction in itself, because of its grand size and the finely finished cherry wood that is intricately carved and highlighted with brightly polished brass. Greek Prawns are a favorite at "Teddy's," and with this recipe you can make as few or as many as you need!

Prawns
Fresh Basil leaves
Pancetta Bacon
olive oil

Rinse prawns under cold water and drain. Split prawns open and place a basil leaf on top of each prawn. Leaving each prawn open, wrap with the Pancetta, covering most of the prawn. Brush with olive oil. Grill until prawn is cooked through (about 3 minutes).

Wild Rice Pilaf

This side dish can be in the oven baking while your guests arrive. If you have a roast in the oven at the same time, all you'll need to do is dress a green salad and enjoy time with your guests!

1/2 cup margarine
1/2 cup slivered almonds
2 tablespoons chopped chives
1/2 pound mushrooms, sliced
1 cup wild rice
3 cups chicken broth

Preheat oven to 350°. Melt margarine in a heavy skillet. Cook the almonds, chives, mushrooms and rice over medium heat for 10 minutes, stirring constantly. Transfer to a greased casserole and add chicken broth. Cover and cook for 2 hours at 350°.

In the late 1880's the Hinman brothers homesteaded 160 acres of forested land and adjoining waterfront. They also established a store and a Post Office close by and called the town, Clinton. The men built a dock and quickly established the business of supplying the needs of the steamers coming to Whidbey Island. The Hinmans stayed busy for several years clearing land, hauling wood by ox cart, building boats, and developing a brick yard. Today, the ferry that connects Whidbey to the mainland, operates out of Clinton.

Oven Roasted Chicken with Rosemary and White Wine

Begin your meal with a tasty appetizer from Seabolt's Smokehouse located at Deception Pass State Park on North Whidbey. Jim and Keren Seabolt started their smoked seafood business in 1977 and have delighted customers all over the world with the unbeatable brand of seafood they prepare. They offer Smoked King, Chum, and Coho Salmon as well as Salmon Jerky, Cajun style Salmon, Pickled Salmon and Lox. Be sure to try their Smoked Salmon Paté, an island favorite!

Let the rich aroma of a roasting chicken fill your home while you anticipate this delicious dinner.

1 whole fryer
1 lemon
3 tablespoons olive oil
1 tablespoon butter
2 cloves minced garlic
1 teaspoon dried rosemary
  (or 1 tablespoon chopped fresh)
2 teaspoons snipped parsley
1/4 cup dry white wine
salt and pepper to taste

Preheat oven to 325°. Wash chicken and pat dry. Place in roasting pan and season. Roll lemon on countertop several times to soften. Pierce with a meat fork many times and place the lemon in the cavity of the chicken. Drizzle 2 tablespoons olive oil over chicken. Combine remaining ingredients in a small saucepan and simmer for several minutes. Baste chicken with this mixture while roasting. Bake for 1/2 hours. Remove lemon before serving.

Nothing adds to the Christmas season more than giving something of yourself to others. Spread cheer by gathering a group of musical chums to carol in neighborhoods, senior centers and hospitals. Put the chicken and onions in the oven before you leave and the warm dinner will add to your guests' glowing spirits upon your return.

Holiday Herb Spread

Roasted Red Pepper Dip with
Broccoli and Cauliflower Crudités

Oven Roasted Chicken with Rosemary

Stuffed Onions

Vegetable Medley

Irish Coffee

White Chocolate Macadamia Nut Cookies

Winter Salad

After the busy holiday season, the pace of activity slows and we re-evaluate our eating habits. Winter Salad fits the bill for our New Year's resolution of eating low fat, but flavorful food.

The leaves of celery contain an intense flavor. Don't hesitate to chop them with the stalk and use the whole vegetable in your recipes.

2 pounds (or 3 packages frozen) green beans
3 stalks celery
1 red onion, thinly sliced
1 green pepper, sliced
1 bunch radishes, thinly sliced

Cut the green beans and celery into 1 inch pieces. Blanch green beans in lightly salted boiling water for 3-5 minutes. Drain and rinse in cold water. Combine vegetables in a large bowl. Add Buttermilk Dressing and mix thoroughly. Chill until serving. Serve in a lettuce lined bowl.

Buttermilk Dressing

1/2 cup skim buttermilk
1/4 cup chopped green onion stalks
2 tablespoons chopped red onion
1 teaspoon, each, fresh basil, parsley and thyme
  (If using dried herbs, cut amount in half)
2 cloves minced garlic
salt and pepper to taste

Combine all ingredients and whisk until blended.

Vegetable Medley

Try a different variation of these tried and true vegetable favorites.

4 carrots
3 small zucchini
2 yellow summer squash
4 green onions
juice of 1 lemon
1/4 cup olive oil
1/2 teaspoon dried thyme
salt and pepper to taste

Dice carrots, zucchini, and squash into 1 inch pieces. Cut green onions into 2 inch pieces. In a large pan, place a steamer basket over 1 inch of water. Bring water to a boil and add carrots to the pan. Cover and cook for 4 minutes. Add zucchini, cover and cook for an additional 2 minutes. Add yellow squash and green onions. Steam for an additional 2 minutes. Remove pan from heat. Prepare dressing by combining remaining ingredients in a small jar; shake well. After straining vegetables, place in a serving bowl. Pour dressing over and toss. Serve warm or cold.

Stockpot Seafood

Flavored olive oils have an intriguing, high taste. They are perfect substitutes for margarine and butter in almost all stovetop cooking. Anyone who is interested in fresher, healthier foods will enjoy using the variety of olive oils available at most grocery stores.

Take advantage of the plentiful seafood found in our coastal waters. This is an entreé that will be gratifying no matter what kind of fish you decide to use.

2 cloves minced garlic
2 tablespoons olive oil
1 onion, chopped
4 large stalks chopped celery
1/4 cup chopped green pepper
1/4 cup chopped red pepper
1 teaspoon chicken stock base
1 cup dry white wine
1 (14 1/2 ounce) can chopped tomatoes,
  undrained
1/2 teaspoon salt
1/4 teaspoon pepper
1 bay leaf
1 1/2 pounds skinned fish fillets; such as
  halibut, rockfish, salmon

In a large pot, sauté the onion, celery and peppers in the garlic and olive oil until tender. Whisk the chicken stock base into 1 1/2 cups water and add to the vegetables. Add the wine, tomatoes, and seasonings to the pot. Bring to a boil; cover and reduce heat. Simmer for 20 minutes. Cut the fish into cubed pieces and add to the pot. Simmer for 8-12 minutes. The fish will flake easily when it is cooked. Discard the bay leaf. Serve in large soup bowls with a salad and bread. This is also very tasty when served over white rice.

Leeks in Red Wine

Serve the leeks hot as a side dish or chilled as a salad.

6 fresh leeks
3 tablespoons butter
1 cup red wine
1/2 cup beef broth
salt and pepper to taste
parsley for garnish

Cut leeks into uniform size, about 1 1/2 inch pieces. Melt the butter in a heavy skillet and add leeks. Brown the leeks, turning as needed. Add wine, broth, salt and pepper. Cover and cook over low heat for 8 minutes or until leeks are tender. Remove leeks and continue to simmer broth until it is reduced to 1 cup. Pour reduced sauce over leeks and garnish with parsley.

*In France,
leeks are
known as the
"asparagus of
the poor."*

Pinot Noir Truffles

Visit the island's
family owned
winery, Whidbey
Island Winery,
near Langley.
Greg and
Elizabeth
Osenbach create
wines produced
from estate
Vinifera grapes,
island grown
rhubarb, and
grapes that they
tenderly
care for in their
own vineyard.
The Osenbach's
agree that their
Pinot Noir wine
creates a richness
in our truffle
recipe at right.

This lovely little morsel is quite heavenly due
to the splash of rich red wine.

3 ounces unsweetened chocolate
1/3 cup butter
1 1/4 cups powdered sugar
3 egg yolks
2 tablespoons *Pinot Noir*, or other red wine
1 cup unsweetened cocoa

Melt the chocolate slowly over low heat or
in the microwave, watching carefully so that
it does not burn. Set aside to cool.
In a mixing bowl, cream butter and sugar.
Add egg yolks, one at a time. Beat until
smooth. Stir in cooled chocolate and wine.
Chill 2-3 hours until it is firm enough to
handle. Spread cocoa on a flat surface.
Break off pieces of chocolate and quickly roll
into small balls (shapes may be irregular).
Coat truffles in the cocoa and store them in
the refrigerator.

Irish Coffee

Chase away the winter chill with a drink that will warm your soul.

* Lightly whip heavy cream until it has barely thickened. Set aside.

* Fill your coffee glasses with very hot water to preheat, then empty.

* Pour coffee into the glasses until they are three-quarters full.

* Drop three sugar cubes into each glass and stir until thoroughly dissolved.

* Add a full jigger of Irish Whiskey to each glass.

* Top each glass with cream by pouring it gently over the back of a spoon into the coffee.

Irish Coffee was originally conceived at the Shannon Airport in Ireland. In 1952, a restauranteur from San Francisco worked tirelessly to recreate the perfection of the Irish Coffee for his establishment. No matter how hard he tried he could not get the cream to float until he approached the mayor of San Francisco, a prominent dairy farmer. After much experimentation, they succeeded when they discovered the cream worked best when aged for 48 hours. Irish Coffee was first served in our country at the Buena Vista restaurant and bar in San Francisco.

Praline Parfait

The winter season is conducive to decadent sweets. This parfait is pleasing to the eye as well as the palate, so be sure to use sparkling, clear crystal pieces when presenting this dessert to your family or guests.

2 cups dark corn syrup
1/3 cup sugar
1 cup chopped pecans

Combine all ingredients with 1/3 cup boiling water. Bring to a boil over medium heat. Remove from heat immediately and cool. Spoon Praline sauce over layers of vanilla ice cream or homemade custard.

Bittersweet Fudge Sauce

This fudge sauce also makes a terrific parfait when layered with vanilla ice cream. Try topping the final layer of ice cream with Creme de Menthe and whipped cream.

1 cup cocoa
3/4 cup white sugar
1/2 cup brown sugar
salt
3/4 cup cream
4 ounces unsalted butter
1 teaspoon vanilla

Mix cocoa, both sugars and a pinch of salt in a saucepan.
Add cream and butter. Heat over medium heat, stirring constantly.
As soon as the mixture comes to a boil, remove from the heat and set aside for 5 minutes. Stir in the vanilla.

Chocolate Currant Torte

Chris Skinner made this dessert and surprised us by announcing that it was "sinless chocolate!" This is a luscious chocolate cake with a glossy coating of currant jelly. And, yes, it is low fat!

1 cup sugar
1/2 cup unsweetened cocoa
3 squares (3 ounces) semisweet chocolate
2 tablespoons *Whidbey's* liqueur
1/4 teaspoon vanilla
2 egg yolks
4 egg whites
1/4 teaspoon cream of tartar
3 tablespoons flour
1/4 cup currant jelly

Preheat oven to 375°. In a microwave-proof bowl, combine 3/4 cup sugar and the cocoa. Add 1/2 cup boiling water and stir until smooth. Chop semisweet chocolate and mix in until melted (you may need to microwave this on medium heat for 1 minute). Whisk in liqueur, vanilla and egg yolks. Add the flour last. In a mixing bowl, beat egg whites with cream of tartar to soft peaks. Beat in remaining 1/4 cup sugar until peaks are stiff. Fold half of the whites into the chocolate mixture, then fold in remaining whites. Line the bottom of a 9 inch springform pan with wax paper. Lightly coat with non stick spray. Spoon the batter evenly into the pan. Bake 30 minutes, until a toothpick inserted comes out with moist crumbs. Cool completely on wire rack. Invert cake onto serving platter and peel off paper. Brush with melted jelly. Cover well and refrigerate until serving.

Whidbey's liqueur is produced and bottled at Whidbey's Greenbank Farm using fresh local loganberries. However, Creme de Cassis or brandy can be used as a substitute. If you have Whidbey's on hand, try pouring 2 tablespoons over lemon or berry flavored sorbet served in chilled wine glasses. Offer Whidbey's liqueur chocolates as an extra indulgence. Dessert can't be simpler... or more divine!

White Chocolate Macadamia Nut Cookies

*"It is here,
in the midst
Of Winter's
first song,
That I find
true meaning
And the
peace
for which
I long."*

Brad Zylstra from
"Winter's First Song"

Sweeten a winter afternoon with this flavorful cookie. Savor a cup of tea, read under a big coverlet, and let your dreams blossom as the pulse of nature slows.

1 cup margarine
1/2 cup brown sugar
1 1/2 cups sugar
2 eggs
1/2 teaspoon vanilla
3 cups flour
1 teaspoon, each, baking soda and salt
12 ounces white chocolate baking chips
1 cup macadamia nuts, coarsely chopped

Preheat oven to 325°. Cream butter and sugars until light and fluffy. Add eggs and vanilla and beat for 1 minute on high speed. Add flour, soda and salt; mix until thoroughly combined. Add white chocolate and nuts and mix again. Drop dough by rounded tablespoons onto baking sheet. Slightly flatten each cookie with the back of a spoon. Bake 12 minutes and cool on wire racks.

** To make larger cookies, use a small
ice cream scoop to drop cookies!*

"For The Birds"

"The mellow year is hasting to its close;
The little birds have almost sung their last..."

Hartley Coleridge

Bird Watchers are lured to Whidbey to see
herons, mallards, puffins, American widgeons,
loons, and bald eagles. During the winter,
tundra swans and snow geese are sometimes
spotted. When island residents fill their feeders
in the wintertime they are delighted to see a
host of winged visitors. Stock your feeder with
this sweet mixture "for the birds."

1 cup shortening
2 cups cornmeal
1/2 cup flour
1 cup white or brown sugar
assorted nutmeats

In a saucepan, bring shortening and 6 cups
water to a boil. Add cornmeal, flour, and sugar.
Mix well and remove from heat. Add any extras
such as nutmeats, seeds, or raisins.Cover and
allow to cool completely before placing at
birdfeeders.

*The Whidbey
Island Audubon
Society teaches
birding classes,
leads field trips,
and monitors
environmental
changes that
could directly
affect wildlife
and humans.
They also
subsidize
natural history
classes in the
elementary
schools.*

❦ Spring ❦

"Springtime at the Bush Point Store"

The Bush Point Store is a classic old building with a wood planked floor and a porch often used for just sitting and talking. It was built as the Bush Point Mercantile and General Store sometime between 1929 and 1931. The Farmer family built and operated the store for several generations and supplied the needs of the people working in the logging camp on South Whidbey. In addition to the store, a boathouse was built on the beach nearby for fishing boat rentals.

• •

"Through the clear windows of morning, turn
Thine angel eyes upon our western isle,
Which in full choir hails thy approach, O Spring!"

from "To Spring" by William Blake

• •

List of Recipes ~ Spring

Blueberry Breakfast Bread

Island Tyme Stuffed French Toast

Prosciutto Fontina Cheese Tart

Sweet Red Pepper and Crab Bisque

Bay Scallop Ceviche

Gruyere Baguettes

Sun Dried Tomato Spread

Cider Poached Oysters

Butter Lettuce Salad with Basil Dressing

Marinated Penn Cove Mussels

Scalloped Mushrooms

Shoepeg Corn Salad

Amaretto Curried Chicken

Bell Peppers with Pesto

Seafood Lasagne

Cool Herbed Rice Salad

Pasta with Salmon and Pistachio Pesto

Lemon Chardonnay Cake

Poor Man Squares

Mocha Grinder and Iced Coffee

With busy schedules we tend to put off leisurely affairs. Make a date today! Sit back and bask in the spring sunshine that heralds the arrival of sunny days and easy living.

Sweet Red Pepper and Crab Bisque

Gruyere Baguettes with Sun Dried Tomato Spread

Cool Herbed Rice Salad

Shoepeg Corn Salad

Poor Man Squares

Mocha Grinder

Blueberry Breakfast Bread

North Island Bed and Breakfast provides a quiet escape for weekend guests. Located on the west side of Whidbey, visitors are offered views of the active shipping lanes in the Rosario Straits, migrating whales and spectacular sunsets. Owners, Jim and Maryvern Loomis, make each guest room particularly cozy with a fireplace, down bedding and a private deck. Wake up to a brisk beach walk and Blueberry Breakfast Bread at the North Island B & B.

3 cups blueberries	2 1/2 cups flour
1 1/2 cups sugar	3 teaspoons baking powder
2 tablespoons butter, softened	1/4 teaspoon salt
	1/2 teaspoon cinnamon
1 egg	1 1/2 cups milk

Preheat oven to 400°. Sprinkle 1/2 cup sugar evenly over blueberries and set aside. In a mixing bowl, cream butter with remaining sugar; beat in egg. Sift flour, baking powder, salt and cinnamon together. Add flour mixture and milk, alternately to batter. Blend well. Fold berries into batter. Spread the mixture evenly into a buttered 9 inch square pan. Bake for 25 minutes. Sprinkle with topping; bake for 10 more minutes or until toothpick comes out clean. Cut into squares and cool in pan.

Topping

2 tablespoons melted butter
1/4 cup sugar
1/4 cup flour
2 tablespoons brown sugar
1/4 teaspoon cinnamon

Mix all ingredients together with a fork until crumbly.

Island Tyme Stuffed French Toast

This specialty breakfast is often served in the turret dining room of
the Island Tyme Bed & Breakfast. Tucked away on ten peaceful wooded
acres near Langley, owner's Phil and Lyn Fauth, welcome guests to a
three story country Victorian home. The turned spindles, ruffled
shingles, gingerbread gables and covered porch beckon visitors to come
in and stay awhile. After strolling the grounds and curling up in a room
furnished with oak and pine antiques, most guests find it hard to leave
Island Tyme.

1 (8 ounce) package cream cheese, softened
1 1/2 teaspoon vanilla
3/4 teaspoon sugar
1/2 cup chopped pecans
1 (16 ounce) loaf soft French bread
4 eggs, beaten
1 cup milk
1/2 teaspoon freshly grated nutmeg
1 (12 ounce) jar apricot preserves
1/2 cup orange juice

In a small mixing bowl, beat the cream cheese, 1 teaspoon of the vanilla,
and the sugar until creamy. Stir in the pecans; set aside. Cut bread into
10-12 slices, 1 1/2 inches thick. Cut a slit near the top in each slice,
creating a pocket. Fill each pocket with 1 1/2 tablespoons cream cheese
mixture. Beat eggs, milk, remaining vanilla, and nutmeg in a large
shallow bowl.

Dip both sides of the filled bread slices into egg mixture. Cook on a
lightly greased griddle until both sides are golden brown. Remove to a
platter and warm in a 200° oven until serving. Cook remaining toast.
Heat the preserves and orange juice in a small saucepan. Simmer for
3-4 minutes until slightly thickened. Drizzle the hot apricot sauce over
the French toast and serve.

Prosciutto Fontina Cheese Tart

Create an appetizer masterpiece with flavors of Italy!
Experiment with this recipe using combinations of
different cheeses, roasted peppers, artichoke hearts,
pestos, grilled shrimp or vegetables and pine nuts.
This recipe also makes a nice, light main course.

1 sheet frozen puff pastry, thawed
8 ounces grated Fontina cheese
1/4 pound Proscuitto, cut into small strips
1/2 cup grated Parmesan cheese
1 tablespoon olive oil
1 tablespoon chopped fresh basil
  or 1 teaspoon dried basil

Preheat oven to 375°. Roll out pastry sheet on a
lightly floured surface to a 16 x 12 inch rectangle.
Transfer pastry to a greased baking sheet and gently
press into place. Trim edges of pastry, leaving
1/2 inch overhang. Crimp edges. Pierce pastry with
fork. Bake 15 minutes, piercing with fork every
5 minutes if needed to deflate crust. Remove from
oven and increase oven temperature to 425°.
Sprinkle with Fontina, and lay Proscuitto on top.
Sprinkle Parmesan, oil, and basil overall. Bake
8 minutes. Cool and cut into squares.

*As the
Italians say,
"Mangia...
Que te fa bene!"
("Eat... it's
good for you!")*

Sweet Red Pepper and Crab Bisque

Caryn Riley owned a restaurant in Oak Harbor for several years. Going to her restaurant was like opening the door to the home of an old friend. The warm smells of soups on the stove and bread in the oven beckoned us to enjoy our favorite repasts in country comfort.

2 tablespoons butter
1 cup finely chopped onion
1 cup finely chopped celery
1 cup finely chopped red pepper
1 1/4 teaspoon "Old Bay" seasoning
3 cups fish stock or bottled clam juice
1/2 cup peeled and diced Russet potato
1/2 cup half and half
1 pound crab
salt and pepper to taste

Melt the butter in a large saucepan. Add onion, celery, red pepper and seasoning. Cover pan and cook 10 minutes on medium heat, stirring twice. Add stock or clam juice and potato. Simmer 30 minutes. Pureé half and half and crab in a processor and add to saucepan. Simmer until warm and season to taste.

Bay Scallop Ceviche

Pack our Ceviche into your ice chest and take it along with your picnic basket to watch the activity of the Penn Cove Water Festival!

1 pound bay scallops
7 limes
4 large Roma tomatoes, peeled and finely
   chopped
1/2 cup chopped onion
2 ripe avocados, peeled and diced
2 teaspoons tarragon
1/2 teaspoon oregano
salt to taste

Place the scallops in a bowl and cover with the juice from 6 of the limes. Let marinate for 1 hour. Drain the scallops and pat dry. In a large bowl, combine the scallops with the tomato, onion, avocado and seasonings. Cover with the juice from the remaining lime. Stir through and enjoy as a refreshing appetizer!

Set aside the weekend in May when the historic town of Coupeville celebrates the Penn Cove Water Festival. There is a variety of music and entertainment including Native American drumming, storytelling, and dancing. Enjoy a salmon bake and native foods while you learn how life on an island is interdependent with its surrounding waters. The highlight of the festival each year is the canoe race in the cove between different tribes from our Native American community. This event continues the tradition that was held for many years in the early 1930's.

Gruyere Baguettes

....

Whidbey wildlife watchers often catch a glimpse of gray whales that migrate to the Arctic from California throughout the late spring and early summer. Keen observers will also see river otters, harbor seals, sea lions, and occasionally other kinds of whales. Remember to "Look for the spout!"

....

There is always a place on the table for fresh baguettes.

2 tablespoons packed brown sugar
1 envelope dry yeast
2 1/4 cups white flour
3/4 cup whole wheat flour
2 tablespoons butter
1 1/2 teaspoons salt
2 tablespoons cornmeal
1 1/2 ounce Gruyere cheese, grated
1 egg, beaten with 1/2 teaspoon salt

In a small bowl, combine sugar with 1 cup warm water. Sprinkle yeast over water and stir. Let mixture set for 10 minutes. Combine flours, butter and salt in a large bowl. Add yeast mixture and knead until dough is elastic. Place dough in a large oiled bowl. Invert dough to coat all sides. Cover with plastic wrap and allow to rise in a warm area for 1 1/2 hours or until double in size.

Preheat oven to 400°. Grease a double French loaf pan or baking sheet. Sprinkle with cornmeal. Divide dough into 2 pieces. On a floured surface, roll each piece out to a 10x12 inch rectangle. Sprinkle each piece with cheese and roll in a jelly roll fashion, pinching edges together. Brush with egg. Bake for 15 minutes, then reduce temperature to 350° and bake for 30 minutes longer.

Sun Dried Tomato Spread

Kathy Radosta created this fabulous appetizer to be served on crusty French bread. Make it ahead of time and serve it with a well chilled bottle of *Madeleine Angevine* wine from Whidbey Island Vineyard and Winery. Greg and Elizabeth Osenbach tell us that this grape, from the Loire Valley, grows extremely well in our island climate. It produces a delicate, crisp, and very dry white wine.

3/4 pound sun dried tomatoes (not in oil)
1/2 cup crumbled Feta cheese
2 stalks diced celery
1 diced carrot
1 clove minced garlic
3 minced green onions
1/4 cup olive oil
2 tablespoons "Mutiny Bay Gourmet"
   Chile Pepper vinegar or red wine vinegar

In a small saucepan, cover the tomatoes with water and bring to a boil. Simmer 5 minutes until tomatoes are plump. Drain and pat dry. Place all ingredients in a processor and blend. Or, combine the first 6 ingredients in a large bowl. Whisk oil, vinegar and pepper together and mix through spread.

Long time friends, Marcia Comer and Karen Erskine gave their gourmet vinegars and spices as gifts for years before developing their "Mutiny Bay Gourmet" business. The white wine based vinegars are packed with fresh herbs and are rich in flavor and aroma. They also offer jars of spice blends and an assortment pack of the spices with suggested uses. Marcia and Karen encourage people to use their imagination with their versatile products!

Cider Poached Oysters

*People generally have
strong opinions about
oysters. They either love
to eat them right out of
the water smacking their
lips in glee, or they
instantly form a look of
disgust at the mere
mention of an oyster.
We have a variety of
oysters that come from
different growing regions
on the West Coast.
When preparing oysters,
remember that the
less time an oyster has
spent away from its
native waters, the more
succulent its flavor will
be. Once they are
gathered they should
be stored in a cool,
dark place to assure that
they keep their shells
tightly closed. (Don't
try to keep oysters in
"salty water" unless
it is real sea water.)*

Kasteel Franssen is a beautiful restaurant located in Oak Harbor. Its design comes from the castles in the south of Holland. The restaurant is easily recognizable with its large water wheel in the front of the building. The adjacent hotel, The Auld Holland Inn, has a grand windmill that bids guests to stay and enjoy a blend of Northwest and European cuisine in the understated elegance of Kasteel. Chef Scott Fraser created this recipe for those who appreciate the most delicate of shellfish, the oyster.

24 pre-shucked medium sized oysters
8 ounces Martinelli's sparkling cider
juice from 1 lemon
1 teaspoon chopped shallots
1 teaspoon finely chopped parsley
4 tablespoons cold, hard butter
salt and pepper to taste

In a medium sized sauté pan, bring cider, lemon and shallots to a boil. Add shucked oysters and simmer 2 minutes until they firm up. Remove oysters and reduce liquid by half. Add parsley and butter, a little at a time, so the butter binds with the liquid to make a smooth sauce. Season with salt and pepper. Add oysters back to the pan and warm them in the sauce. Serve with a French baguette.

Butter Lettuce Salad with Basil Dressing

A crisp green salad is an easy accompaniment to any main dish. Running short of time? Take advantage of the selection of gourmet salad dressings in your local market. The citrus or berry vinaigrettes are excellent with this salad. Add oranges or raspberries to the butter lettuce to compliment the vinaigrette. You'll receive rave reviews!

Basil, with its heart shaped leaves and stimulating flavor, represents love in Italy.

1 head Butter lettuce
1/2 red onion, sliced into rings
1/4 cup pine nuts
1 avocado, sliced thin
3 Roma tomatoes
1/4 cup crumbled Gorgonzola cheese

Tear lettuce into bite size pieces. Cut tomatoes into small pieces. Add onion, pine nuts, tomatoes, avocado and cheese to the lettuce. Pour the dressing over all and toss lightly.

Basil Dressing

1/4 cup red wine vinegar
1/2 cup extra virgin olive oil
2 teaspoons sugar
1 clove minced garlic
2 tablespoons fresh, minced basil
  (or 1 tablespoon dried)

Combine all ingredients and add to salad just before serving.

Marinated Penn Cove Mussels

This is a favorite recipe given to us by the owners of Penn Cove Mussels, Inc. Serve the marinated mussels hot with a bowl of steaming broth or chilled for an easy appetizer.

Storage: Store mussels in the refrigerator and cover with a damp cloth or ice. Drain liquid as they should not stand in water. Leave the mussel beard intact until 2 hours before serving.

Preparation: Within a couple hours of cooking, remove the mussel beard by giving it a sharp pull toward the pointed end of the shell. Lightly rinse mussels under running water. Discard any that will not try to stay closed after squeezing the shell shut.

5 pounds Penn Cove Mussels
1/2 cup dry white wine
1/4 cup chopped scallions or shallots
2 cloves minced garlic
1 tablespoon chopped parsley
1 tablespoon herbs of choice (basil, tarragon, etc...)
4 tablespoons butter

Place all ingredients, except mussels, in a large pan over high heat and bring to a boil. Add mussels and cover pan. Steam 5-6 minutes or until shells are open and meats are not translucent. Remove mussels from broth and set aside in a large bowl in the refrigerator to cool in their shells.

*Continued on next page

Marinade

• •

1/2 gallon cider vinegar
2 1/2 cups sugar
1/2 sliced red onion
2 tablespoons pimentos
3 cloves minced garlic

The vinegar to sugar mixture should be a
3:1 ratio; or enough to cover the mussels.
Stir the sugar with the cider vinegar until
completely dissolved. Add the onion,
scallions, pimento, and garlic. Pour the
marinade over the top of the bowl of
mussels only after the mussels have cooled
completely. Drain marinade from bowl
and pour over mussels several times until
all mussels are soaked. Cover bowl and
keep cool until mussels are to be used.

Mussels should sit in marinade at least an
hour before serving and may be kept in
marinade up to a week. Pour marinade
over mussels right before serving. Serve
alone, or as an accompaniment to pasta
and salad.

Appetizers for 6-10 people

Penn Cove
Mussel Inc.,
started by the
Jefferds family,
operates from
Penn Cove, an
idyllic spot
located in the
central part of
Whidbey Island.
They provide
islanders and
establishments all
over the country,
with mussels grown
from their rafts.
However you
choose to showcase
our region's
specialty, you will
be serving the
purest gourmet
shellfish Whidbey
has to offer.

Scalloped Mushrooms

This is a recipe for those of you who love mushrooms as much as we do!

1 1/2 pounds mushrooms, sliced
3 cups bread crumbs
3/4 cup butter, melted
salt and pepper to taste
1/2 cup dry white wine

Preheat oven to 325°. In a buttered 2 quart casserole dish, layer 1/3 of the mushrooms, 1/3 of the crumbs, and drizzle 1/3 of the butter over all. Season to taste. Repeat layers. Finish with a layer of mushrooms and pour the wine over all. Cover and bake for 35 minutes. Combine any remaining butter and crumbs to spoon over the mushrooms and bake, uncovered, for 10 more minutes.

In order to preserve and protect the unique marine environment on Whidbey Island, Washington State University trains volunteer "Beachwatchers." Each volunteer adopts a section of beach to monitor on a regular basis. In addition, each volunteer is expected to spend 50 hours a year sharing their knowledge on water quality educational and action projects.

Spend a spring afternoon exploring the art galleries on Whidbey Island. Even if you don't purchase a piece, you can observe the wide variety of art that is available on our island and perhaps meet the artists themselves.

Proscuitto Fontina Cheese Tart

Bell Peppers with Pesto

Pasta with Salmon and Pistachio Pesto

Butter Lettuce Salad with Basil Dressing

Island White Wine from Whidbey Island Winery

Lemon Chardonnay Cake

Shoepeg Corn Salad

Oak Harbor is home to the Whidbey Island Naval Air Station, a fairly large military base. Thus, North Whidbey residents hail from many places across the country. Valerie Wallace shared this recipe from her home state of Texas. It is sensational!

2 (11 ounce) cans shoepeg (white) corn, drained
1/4 cup chopped green pepper
2 tablespoons diced pimento
1/2 cup chopped celery
1 cup peeled and thinly sliced cucumber
1/2 cup thinly sliced red onion

Dressing

1/3 cup vegetable oil
3 tablespoons sugar
1 1/2 teaspoons salt
3 tablespoons red wine vinegar

Combine ingredients for dressing and shake well. Place all vegetables in a bowl and add dressing. Toss gently, cover and chill for 8 - 10 hours. Drain before serving.

Amaretto Curried Chicken

When you throw open the door to your home and embrace your friends, it does something for your heart. Some people say they are not comfortable entertaining, wouldn't know what to fix, or how to do it in an appealing manner. With an entreé like this one, you'll be assured of a recipe that is easy to understand and one that can be done ahead of time. Complete this dish with a steamed fresh vegetable dashed with parmesan, and serve a green salad. You're ready for your entertaining debut!

6 boneless chicken breasts, skinned
3/4 cup flour
2 teaspoons curry powder
1 1/2 teaspoons garlic powder
1/4 cup butter
3/4 pound mushrooms, thickly sliced
1/4 cup Amaretto liqueur
juice and grated rind of 1 lemon
1 1/3 cups chicken broth
1 tablespoon cornstarch
salt and white pepper for seasoning

Cut chicken into bite size pieces. Combine flour and curry powder. Roll pieces in flour mixture. Heat butter in a large skillet. Brown chicken pieces on all sides. Add mushrooms, Amaretto, lemon juice and rind. Simmer 5 minutes. In a small bowl, mix chicken broth and cornstarch. Stir into skillet. Stir over low heat until mixture bubbles and thickens. Season with salt and white pepper. Serve over cooked rice.

Set a splendid table by first covering it with a cloth or a sheet. Pin tassels on the corners. Create a pool of light with candles in all sizes and shapes. Arrange a bunch of wild flowers in little vases or jars up and down the table. Lay several blooms on the table wrapped in lacy paper doilies. Roll your napkins in colored ribbons tied in bows or use a different napkin ring for each setting. You can even toss some silver wrapped chocolate kisses on your table for a romantic touch! Dim the lights, turn on soft music and enjoy every moment.

Bell Peppers
with Basil

Sunnyside
Cemetery is
situated on a hill
overlooking
Ebey's prairie.
The land was
donated by
Jacob Ebey and
contains plots
belonging to
many pioneer
families.
A visit to the
cemetery is like
a walk through
Coupeville's
history.

Multi-colored bell peppers are an unusual and colorful compliment to many entreés. This recipe can be prepared a day ahead, which makes it very appealing to the busy hostess.

3 bell peppers; red, yellow, green or orange
1 onion
2 tablespoons oil
1/4 cup vinegar
salt and pepper to taste
2 teaspoons basil

Slice peppers and onion into 1/2 inch wide pieces. Heat oil in a heavy skillet over medium heat. Add peppers and onion and cook until peppers are softened, about 5 minutes. Place in a serving bowl. Add vinegar, basil, and season with salt and pepper. Refrigerate until well chilled.

Seafood Lasagna

We often consult our friend, Liz Kline, when we are searching for a unique dish. This seafood entreé received rave reviews at a recent party.

1/2 pound lasagna noodles
1 pint cottage cheese
2 (8 ounce) packages cream cheese
1/2 cup minced onion
1 egg, beaten
2 teaspoons dry basil
1 teaspoon pepper
2 (10 1/2 ounce) cans cream of shrimp soup
1 cup flaked fresh crab
1 (6 1/2 ounce) can tuna, drained
4 sliced tomatoes
2 teaspoons sugar
1 cup grated Parmesan cheese

"Life is nothing without friendship."

Cicero

Cook noodles and drain thoroughly. In a large bowl, combine cream cheese, onion, egg, basil, cottage cheese, salt and pepper. Blend well and set aside. In a saucepan, heat soup until bubbling; stir in crab and tuna. Preheat oven to 375°. Arrange half the noodles in a greased 9 x 13 inch baking dish. Cover with half the cheese mixture. Top with all of the seafood sauce. Cover with remaining noodles and cheese mixture. Arrange tomatoes on top and sprinkle with sugar. Bake for 20 minutes. Sprinkle with Parmesan and continue baking for 30 minutes or until hot.

Cool Herbed
Rice Salad

Fresh herbs, shrimp, pine nuts, tomatoes and Feta cheese create a Mediterranean flair in this delicious salad.

1 1/2 cups white rice
1 teaspoon minced garlic
1/4 teaspoon salt
1/4 teaspoon white pepper
1 teaspoon, each, snipped parsley, chives, basil and thyme
1/4 cup olive oil
1 cup chopped tomato
1/2 pound small shrimp, cooked and cooled
1 cup crumbled Feta cheese

In a large saucepan, bring 3 cups water to a boil. Add rice, garlic, salt and pepper. Bring to a rapid boil, cover and reduce to low heat. Simmer for 20 minutes, remove from heat and keep covered for 10 minutes. Place rice in a large bowl and allow to cool completely. Add fresh herbs and oil and mix thoroughly. Gently toss in tomato and shrimp. Top with Feta.

Pasta with Salmon and Pistachio Pesto

"L'Approdo Cucina Italiana" is a lovely Italian restaurant located in Oak Harbor. Once inside, patrons will feel as though they are sitting in a private Italian patio surrounded by blooming flowers and trailing vines. The interior walls are soft colored murals painted by a local artist. Pasta with Salmon is an elegant entreé created for "L'Approdo."

16 ounces angel hair pasta
2 pounds salmon, deboned, including pinbones
Pecorino Romano cheese

Slice salmon into half inch pieces on the bias. Grill or broil salmon on each side until it is just transparent. Brush top with Pistachio Pesto and let salmon finish cooking. Set the salmon on top of the pasta and top with Pecorino Romano.

Pistachio Pesto

2 cups firmly packed fresh basil leaves	**3/4 cup Pecorino Roman cheese**
1/2 cup pistachio nuts	**1/2 cup olive oil**
3 cloves garlic	

Wash basil leaves and dry completely between paper towels. In a blender or processor, whirl basil, nuts and garlic until pureéd. Blend in cheese. With machine on low speed, pour oil in slowly to blend. (If not serving immediately, cover pesto with a thin layer of olive oil to prevent darkening.) Refrigerate.

Determining whether a fish is fully cooked can be a little intimidating, but easy to observe. As the fish cooks, the layers of flesh become less firmly attached and push apart easily. The fish flakes when prodded. This separation starts on the surface and works inward. Heat equalizes for a few minutes after the fish comes off the grill.

Lemon Chardonnay Cake

Vicky O'Kelley assured us her cake recipe was something extraordinary and worth saving for a special occasion, which is exactly what we did. We found it has a subtle, yet distinctive lemon tang and each bite of this tall, layered cake literally melted in our mouths! Prepare the Lemon Curd first so it can cool while you prepare the cake.

Lemon Curd

· ·

7/8 cup butter
3/4 cup sugar
juice of 2 lemons, and zest of 1 lemon
3 egg yolks
2 whole eggs

In a small saucepan, bring butter, sugar, lemon juice and zest to a boil. In a small bowl, whip egg yolks and eggs together. Add a bit of the boiled mixture to the eggs. Then, add this back to the boiled mixture in the saucepan. Stir over medium heat and cook until thick, or until the mixture coats the spoon. Cover and chill.

Lemon Cake

· ·

2 1/4 cups sugar
4 eggs
1 cup salad oil
1 cup Chardonnay or white table wine
1 teaspoon vanilla
3 cups flour
2 teaspoons baking powder
1/2 teaspoon salt

Preheat oven to 350°. With a mixer at low speed, combine sugar, eggs and oil. Stir in wine and vanilla. Mix in flour, baking powder and salt. Do not over mix. Pour cake into a greased and floured, 10 inch pan. Bake for 20-30 minutes, until cake springs back to touch. Cool.

continued on next page

Lemon Cream Cheese Icing

3 (8 ounce) packages cream cheese
2 cups powdered sugar
1 1/2 teaspoons vanilla
1 cup butter (at room temperature)
lemon extract or fresh juice to taste

Cream the cream cheese, sugar and vanilla until smooth. Add butter in bits and the lemon; whip until creamy. Set aside.

Simple Syrup

In a saucepan, over medium high heat, boil 1 cup sugar with 2 cups water. Allow to cool.

Cake Assembly

Split the cake into 3 even layers. Brush the top of one cake layer with the Simple Syrup. Place a layer of Lemon Curd on top of the syrup. Spread Cream Cheese Icing on top of curd. Place the next cake layer on top and repeat process of spreading syrup, lemon curd and icing on the cake. Repeat with the third cake layer. Lastly, spread cream cheese icing around the sides of the cake. Enjoy!

Visit the Meerkerk Rhododendron Gardens in Greenbank during their spring blooming season which occurs between March and May. There are more than 50 acres of magnificent rhododendrons and companion plants. The Gardens host a series of special events each year such as their Spring Opening Celebration, a Mayflower Garden Party, and Mother's Day at Meerkerk, complete with live music and demonstrations.

Poor Man Squares

Celebrate the opening day of yachting season at the Oak Harbor Marina. It provides moorage for 420 boats and is a favorite stopping place for boaters cruising toward the San Juan and Canadian Gulf Islands. The Oak Harbor Marina has become well known across the country since sailing skippers and crews look forward to the annual Whidbey Island Race Week.

This is a simple, satisfying snack that can be prepared on your stovetop and baked on a cookie sheet.

1 cup raisins
1 teaspoon soda
1/4 pound margarine
1 cup sugar
1 egg
1/2 teaspoon, each, salt, cloves, allspice, ginger and nutmeg
1 teaspoon cinnamon
2 cups flour
1 cup chopped walnuts

Preheat oven to 350°. In a large saucepan, add 1 cup water to the raisins. Boil for 4 minutes and remove from heat. In order listed above, add the rest of the ingredients to the pan, mixing well to combine thoroughly. Add the nuts, if desired. Spread batter on a cookie sheet. Bake for 15-20 minutes.

Icing

1 cup powdered sugar
2 tablespoons milk

1 tablespoon butter
1 teaspoon vanilla

Mix until smooth and drizzle over spice cake immediately after removing from oven.

Mocha Grinder

People in Oak Harbor flock to the Daily Grind in the summertime for their daily dose of caffeine. Andrea Knoll created the Mocha Grinder that is chilly, chocolatey and completely decadent! It's a must to keep you going through a hot afternoon! When you stop in at the Daily Grind, be sure to take some extra time to browse around the adjoining Book Gallery. They have a large selection of new and used hardcover and paperback books.

1 (2 ounce) shot chilled espresso
3 tablespoons Hershey's syrup
2 tablespoons powdered non-dairy creamer
1 cup milk
1 1/2 cups ice

Combine all ingredients in a blender. Blend approximately 3 minutes or until it reaches a smooth consistency. If desired, add flavored syrups or shots of espresso for variety.

According to one legend, monks observed how lively the sheep acted after eating coffee cherries. Eventually, the monks began eating the beans to help them stay awake during long nights of prayer. From the "experiment" came our modern day coffee drinks.

Iced Coffee

Quench your mid-day thirst with another coffee favorite!

Brew 1 1/2 cups coffee. When cooled, fill a blender half full with ice and pour in coffee. Add 1 teaspoon sugar, and 1 teaspoon vanilla. Blend until thick and frosty. Serve with a cinnamon stick.

❦ Summer ❦

"Summer Weekend on Whidbey"

Gaze through a window of one of the many Victorian homes located in Coupeville and take a look at Whidbey's past. In 1852 Captain Thomas Coupe founded Coupeville, the second oldest town in the state of Washington. It is here that you will find Coupe's original home built in 1833, the blockhouses built by early settlers as protection against Indian attack, and the Island County Historical Museum. Admire the beauty of Ebey's Landing National Historic Reserve which encompasses 22 square miles of cultural landscape and 91 nationally registered historic structures. Enjoy the warmth and charm of strolling Front street and greeting the people who treasure this very special place.

· ·

"They come! The merry summer months of
beauty, song, and flowers;
The grass is soft, its velvet touch is grateful to
the hand..."

William Motherwell
from "They Come! The Merry Summer Months!"

· ·

List of Recipes ~ Summer

Low fat Peach and Blueberry Muffins
Bacchus Eggs
Friday Frittata
Sherried Creamed Eggs and Mushrooms on Toast
Cantaloupe Rum Soup
Picnic Popovers
Tortilla Chicken Bites with Blue Cheese Dip
Keystone Shell Salad
Mussels Sambouca
Tomato Herb Tart
Chicken Pizza
The Magic of Marinade!
Honey Glazed Salmon
Shaggy Dogs
Jade Tree Salad
Fraser Clams Szechwan
Red Potato and Snap Pea Salad
Grilled Shrimp
Pineapple Red Onion Salsa
Lemon Basil Capellini
Captain Whidbey Ginger Steamed Mussels
Whidbey's Coffee Cheesecake
Summertime Raspberry Cake
Summer Thirst Quenchers

*Although Whidbey sailors and boat owners
are seen on surrounding waters throughout
the year, summer is definitely the season that
boaters enjoy the most. Try this festive meal on
your boat or at one of Whidbey's many parks.*

Fresh Squeezed Orange Juice

Champagne and Whidbey's Coffee

Bacchus Eggs

Cantaloupe Rum Soup

Low fat Peach and Blueberry Muffins

Summertime Raspberry Cake

Low fat Peach and Blueberry Muffins

Some things just feel right: walking in the Northwest drizzle, deeply inhaling a salt air breeze, sleeping until noon on the weekend and waking up to the sweet aroma of baking muffins. Andrea Knoll created this recipe for the Daily Grind in Oak Harbor. Many devoted customers visit this establishment each day for plump muffins full of berries and fruit, a great espresso, and a warm welcome.

2 cups flour
1 cup sugar
2 teaspoons baking powder
1/2 teaspoon salt
1/2 cup non fat milk
1/2 cup applesauce
1 egg
1 teaspoon vanilla
1 cup fresh or frozen blueberries (or other berries)
1 cup chopped fresh or frozen peaches

Preheat oven to 400°. Stir the dry ingredients together in a large bowl, making a well in the center. In a separate bowl, stir together the liquid ingredients. Add this mixture to the dry ingredients and stir until combined. Mix the fruit into the batter. Spoon batter into greased muffin cups (12 regular size or 6 jumbo cups). Sprinkle the tops of the muffins with sugar. Bake 25 minutes and allow to cool 5 minutes before removing muffins from cups. Serve warm, or cool completely before storing them in an airtight container at room temperature. They also freeze well.

The best part of all – each muffin contains less than 1 gram of fat!

Bacchus Eggs

It's easy to make your weekend morning something special when you serve Blueberry Peach Muffins and Bacchus Eggs together. Julienne cantaloupe on each plate and pour orange juice into tall stemware!

In a bowl, whip 3 eggs per person with 1/3 cup light cream. Cut 4 ounces of cream cheese into small pieces and mix in with the eggs. Add dill, salt, pepper and fresh chives to taste. Cook in a skillet as desired.

Julienne means to cut into thin match like strips.

Friday Frittata

Choose your favorite vegetables to add to this easy egg dish that can be used for brunch, lunch or a light supper.

2 cups chopped vegetables such as zucchini, onion, bell peppers, artichoke hearts, spinach, broccoli or mushrooms
2 tablespoons olive oil
12 eggs
1 cup light cream
salt and pepper to taste
1 teaspoon herbes de Provence
3 tablespoons Parmesan cheese
1 tablespoon chopped parsley

Preheat oven to 350°. In a large pan, sauté chopped vegetables in oil just until tender. Transfer vegetables to a large pie plate. Beat eggs and cream together. Add seasonings. Pour cream mixture over vegetables and sprinkle with cheese and parsley. Bake for 15 minutes, or until eggs are fully set.

Sherried Creamed Eggs and Mushrooms on Toast

Twickenham House is a beautiful bed and breakfast inn, in Langley, owned by Maureen and Ray Cooke. The Inn is filled with French pine antique furniture the Cookes purchased in Canada and Europe. This B & B is particularly unique because it has an authentic British Pub. The Pub is the "socializing room," since breakfast and dinner are served to guests in the formal dining room.

2 pounds fresh, sliced mushrooms
1/2 cup plus 2 tablespoons butter
2 tablespoons olive oil
garlic salt to taste
9 tablespoons flour
4 cups whipping cream
1 teaspoon nutmeg
salt and pepper to taste
1 1/2 cups dry sherry
fresh chopped parsley
12 hard boiled eggs, sliced
French bread, sliced thick and toasted

Sauté the mushrooms in 2 tablespoons butter and the olive oil. Season with garlic salt and set aside. In a large skillet, melt remaining 1/2 cup butter. Whisk in the flour and add cream, seasonings, and sherry. Simmer until thickened, stirring occasionally with a wire whisk to keep the sauce smooth. Use a rubber spatula to fold the egg slices and mushrooms into the sherry sauce. Spoon the Sherried Creamed Eggs and Mushrooms over the toasted bread. Garnish the top of each serving with paprika and an orange twist. Place fresh strawberry slices and a sprig of parsley on the side.

12 servings

A breakfast at Twickenham House is always something special. The Cookes prepare Brandied Peaches, Sherried Creamed Eggs and Mushrooms on Toast with English Banger Sausage, and English Scones with Loganberry Sauce topped with Chantilly Creme.

Cantaloupe Rum Soup

"If thou art
wise, lay thee
down now
and steep
thyself in a
bowl of
summer-time."

Virgil

Even on Whidbey we have a few days when it's too warm to cook. This colorful and refreshing soup is just right for those days.

1/2 cup butter
4 ripe cantaloupes
1/2 cup orange marmalade
4 tablespoons unsweetened coconut milk
1 1/2 cups orange juice
juice of 2 lemons
1/2 cup rum
1 cup heavy cream

Peel, seed and cube the cantaloupes. Add fruit to melted butter in a heavy saucepan. Cook over medium heat for 5 minutes. Add marmalade, coconut milk, orange and lemon juices. Stir well. Lower heat and allow to simmer for 10 - 15 minutes, or until cantaloupe is soft. Blend mixture in blender or food processor and return to pan. Add rum and cream. At this point, soup can be rewarmed or refrigerated. Serve warm or chilled; garnish with fresh mint leaves.

Picnic Popovers

We like the versatility of this charming little treat. They make a delightful snack for your picnic on one of Whidbey's beaches. Or, they will make an elegant, warm hors d'oeuvre to share with special dinner guests.

1/2 cup grated Gruyere or Swiss cheese
2 1/2 tablespoons butter
1/2 teaspoon salt
1/4 teaspoon white pepper
1/4 teaspoon nutmeg
1/2 cup flour
2 eggs, at room temperature

Preheat oven to 425°. In a saucepan, bring 1/2 cup water, butter, salt, pepper and nutmeg to a boil. Remove from heat. Add the flour and beat with a wooden spoon until the mixture forms a ball away from sides of pan. Add cheese and mix until incorporated. Beat in the eggs, one at a time, until mixture is smooth. Drop by spoonfuls onto a greased cookie sheet. Sprinkle tops with grated cheese, if desired. Bake for 20 minutes until golden.
This recipe can easily be doubled as the popovers will keep for a few days in the refrigerator when tightly sealed.

Greenbank was founded as a logging community in 1906. The 100 acre loganberry farm was planted a few years later and is still the world's largest loganberry farm. Each July, Whidbey's Farm and Winery celebrates the Loganberry Festival drawing thousands of people to the farm. Those who attend will delight in the musical entertainment, the arts and crafts booths, and the loganberry pie eating contest. There is an outdoor picnic area, wine tasting, and many food vendors to satisfy most cravings on a warm summer day.

Tortilla Chicken Bites

Give your meal a "kick" when you soak chicken strips in a mesquite marinade, an ingredient that gives this appetizer a woodsy flavor.

4 boneless chicken breasts
2 tablespoons mesquite marinade
1 1/2 tablespoons cornstarch
2 tablespoons oil
1 (4 ounce) can diced green chilies
1/2 cup grated jack cheese
Flour Tortillas
Salsa and Blue Cheese Dip

Blend marinade and cornstarch together. Cut chicken into 2 inch pieces, add to the marinade mixture, and toss until chicken is well coated. Let sit for at least 15 minutes. Add oil to a skillet and sauté chicken until cooked. (The marinade will thicken.) Warm the tortillas and cut them into quarters. Assemble as follows: Place 2-3 pieces of chicken onto a tortilla corner. Sprinkle with chilies, cheese, and salsa as desired. Roll and secure with a toothpick. Tortilla Chicken Bites can be served warm or cold. If you make them early in the day, they can easily be reheated. Serve with bowls of salsa and Blue Cheese Dip.

Blue Cheese Dip

1/3 cup crumbled Blue cheese
1/3 cup mayonnaise
1/3 cup sour cream
1/4 teaspoon hot pepper sauce

In a small bowl, add 2 tablespoons boiling water to the cheese and stir until almost smooth. Mix in the mayonnaise, sour cream and hot sauce. Chill until serving.

This is also great when used as a topping for baked potatoes!

Keystone Shell Salad

This salad is a great "take along" dish since it can be made several days in advance, and travels well.

1 (16 ounce) can garbanzo beans
1 (16 ounce) can black beans
1 (16 ounce) red kidney beans
1/2 cup celery, sliced
1/4 cup green pepper, diced
1/2 cup red pepper, diced
1/4 cup green onions, chopped
4 cups large shell macaroni, cooked

Combine beans, vegetables and macaroni.
Toss with dressing and refrigerate overnight.

Dressing

1/3 cup white wine vinegar
1/2 cup rice wine vinegar
1/3 cup vegetable oil
1/2 cup sugar
1 teaspoon, each, salt and pepper

Combine all ingredients in a small jar and shake well.

8 servings

Keystone lies on the west side of Central Whidbey. It is the location for the ferry landing to Port Townsend and the Olympic Peninsula. It is also the location of a well preserved marine park that is extremely popular with scuba divers. Divers encounter a vast assortment of sea life, including multiple species of invertebrates, fish and octopi.

Mussels Sambouca

The Cascadia Marine Trail in Puget Sound is a 150 mile water trail that stretches from Canada to Olympia, Washington. Island County provides many of the shore "rest sites" for paddlers, each site spaced about a day's paddle from the next. There are quite a few B & B's that either have docks for kayaks or provide shuttle vans from the rest site to their inn.

Chef Ben Holden created this recipe for "L'Approdo", an Italian restaurant in Oak Harbor. After 30 years as a chef, Ben considers Italian food his specialty. He acquired a passion for Southern Italian food while studying with a Sicilian chef. Lacing the steamed mussels with Sambouca is a creative way to prepare them.

4 pounds mussels
4 tablespoons sun dried tomatoes
1 teaspoon minced garlic
1 tablespoon olive oil
Sambouca or Anisette liqueur

Rinse and debeard mussels for cooking. In a large pan, reconstitute tomatoes in boiling water for 1 minute. Set aside, leaving them in the water. In a small skillet, heat 1 tablespoon olive oil; add garlic. Sauté for 2 minutes. Put the mussels and garlic oil into the pan with water and tomatoes. Drizzle the top of mussels with Sambouca or Anisette and 2 tablespoons water. Season with salt and pepper. Cover pan and steam until mussels open. Discard any mussels that do not open. Serve in bowls with the broth.

4 appetizer servings

Tomato Herb Tart

Weekends of turning soil and planting now yield in your first luscious tomatoes. Sit in your garden and sample a few right from the vine and then try our tart with its cheesy herb filling. It is an "all occasion" dish that will be lovely for a special brunch or equally appropriate as a side dish to an evening supper.

1 9 inch pie shell, pre-baked 5 minutes
3 medium tomatoes, sliced in 1/2 inch rounds
salt and pepper to taste
1 tablespoon olive oil
1 clove garlic, minced
1 medium onion, finely chopped
4 tablespoons grated Parmesan cheese
2 eggs
1 cup milk
1/2 cup grated Jack cheese
2 tablespoons, each, chopped basil, parsley
  and chives

Preheat oven to 350°. Drain tomato slices on paper towels. Season with salt and pepper. In a skillet, heat oil and sauté garlic and onion until softened. Remove from heat and cool. Sprinkle half of the Parmesan cheese over pie shell. Top with onions. Layer tomato slices on top of onions. In a bowl, beat eggs well. Add milk, cheese and herbs. Pour over the tomatoes. Top with remaining cheese. Bake 35 minutes. Let cool 10 minutes before cutting.

For a bold burst of flavor try baking cherry tomatoes or sliced Roma tomatoes in 1/2 cup vodka spiced with salt, pepper and a minced garlic clove. Bake at 350° for 8 minutes.

Always store tomatoes at room temperature since refrigeration dulls the taste. When you are ready to use the tomatoes, cut them, sprinkle with salt, toss lightly and let them stand. This will help draw out excess water, thus, intensifying the flavor - especially when tomatoes are out of season.

Chicken Pizza

This pizza is easy to prepare and perfect for most summertime occasions. Our friend, Joyce Acheson suggests serving it with a plate of fresh fruit and a crisp green salad.

1 (16 ounce) loaf frozen bread, thawed
1 beaten egg
1 tablespoon olive oil
1/2 pound chicken cut in small pieces
1 small onion
1 small yellow pepper, cut in thin strips
1/4 teaspoon lemon pepper
1/4 cup basil pesto
3 Roma tomatoes, sliced
6 ounces Mozzarella, sliced

Preheat oven to 400°. Roll out thawed loaf and divide into 4 parts. Form 4 circles, approximately 4 inches in diameter. Brush flattened loaves with beaten egg. Bake crusts in oven for 12 - 15 minutes. Sauté chicken and vegetables, season with lemon pepper. Spread crusts with pesto, vegetable chicken mixture and sliced tomatoes. Cover with cheese. Bake an additional 10-15 minutes.

Don a large, straw hat, pack your picnic basket and head for Coupeville's Town Park. On summer weekends you can enjoy a variety of musical troupes with Penn Cove's water activity as a backdrop.

Sparkling Orange Iced Tea

Tortilla Chicken Bites with Blue Cheese Dip

Picnic Popovers

Assorted Cheeses

Red Potato and Snap Pea Salad

Grilled Shrimp with Pineapple Red Onion Salsa

Whidbey's Coffee Cheesecake

The Magic of Marinade!

Marinating is the best way to add a terrific boost of flavor to any meat, fish or poultry. With each marinade, combine all ingredients together in a large bowl or pan. Allow chicken or beef to marinate 4-6 hours in the refrigerator, or overnight for extra tenderizing. Fish can be marinated at room temperature for 2 hours, or for longer when placed in the refrigerator. Be sure to use the marinade for basting while grilling or baking!

Whidbey Island Ale Marinade

Langley is home to the Whidbey Island Brewing Company, established in 1992. Their lagers and ales are handcrafted by Island brewers with local well water to create a classic, northwest taste.

2 teaspoons minced garlic	12 ounces lager or ale
1/4 cup fresh lemon juice	1 tablespoon fresh tarragon,
1 teaspoon salt	finely chopped
1 teaspoon pepper	(or, 1 1/2 teaspoons dried tarragon)

St. Martin Marinade

Dark rum, fresh ginger and lime...a bit of the Caribbean!

3/4 cup dark rum	1 tablespoon minced fresh ginger
3/4 cup soy sauce	4 minced garlic cloves
1/2 cup red wine vinegar	1 teaspoon fresh ground pepper
1/2 cup vegetable oil	Juice of 1 lime
2 teaspoons thyme	

Plum Preserve Marinade

You'll receive "two thumbs up" when using this marinade on chicken!

1 cup plum preserves	1/4 cup soy sauce
1/3 cup tarragon or	1 teaspoon ginger
red wine vinegar	1/4 teaspoon red pepper flakes
1/4 cup chopped green onion	

Honey Glazed Salmon

Rick Almberg's specialty in the kitchen is preparing seafood. This is a quick seafood entreé that does not interfere with his busy schedule. We all need recipes like this one!

3 pounds salmon filets
1 cup honey
1/2 cup rice vinegar
cracked pepper
1/4 teaspoon dill

The night before serving, place the salmon in a large baking dish. In a small bowl, mix the honey and vinegar; pour over the salmon. Refrigerate overnight, turning salmon two or three times. When ready to serve, drain marinade. Cut salmon filets into serving pieces. Preheat oven to broil. Place a heavy skillet over a very hot burner until it just begins to smoke. Fry the salmon in the hot skillet for 3 minutes on each side. Remove from skillet and sprinkle the filet pieces with pepper and dill. Place under the broiler, skin side down, for 7 minutes. Serve immediately.

"I love everything that's old; old friends, old times, old manners, old books, old wines."

Oliver Goldsmith

Shaggy Dogs

This is definitely an innovative recipe for an old standard. Nicholas Juhl experimented with this idea and then named the potatoes, "Shaggy Dogs." The finished product will explain why!

6 medium potatoes, peeled and quartered
1/2 cup grated Parmesan cheese
1 (3 ounce) package cream cheese
2 tablespoons margarine
1 tablespoon chopped chives
1 tablespoon dry onion soup mix
1 tablespoon chopped parsley
1/4 teaspoon pepper
1 egg, beaten
3 cups coarsely crushed corn flakes

Boil potatoes in lightly salted water until tender. Drain and mash. Preheat oven to 400°. Mix in Parmesan, cream cheese, margarine, chives, soup mix, parsley and pepper. Shape potatoes into balls, using approximately 3 tablespoons of potatoes for each ball. Roll each ball in the beaten egg and then in the crushed flakes. Arrange balls on a greased baking sheet and bake for 15 minutes.

Jade Tree Salad

This is a superb luncheon salad given to us by Jill Skinner.
When garnished with avocado and orange slices or grapes it is
especially outstanding.

2 heads romaine lettuce
5 chicken breasts, cooked and shredded
2 cans water chestnuts, drained and sliced
1/4 cup sesame seeds, toasted
1/2 cup Parmesan cheese, grated
Garnish: avocado slices, orange slices and grapes

Tear the lettuce into bite size pieces. Combine all ingredients
in a large bowl and toss. Pour dressing over the salad, toss and
garnish according to taste.

Dressing

1 1/3 cups vegetable oil
2/3 cup tarragon vinegar
2 teaspoons salt
1 teaspoon dry mustard
1/2 teaspoon garlic powder
1/2 teaspoon black pepper
1/4 cup sugar

Combine all ingredients in a jar and shake thoroughly.

Fraser Clams Szechwan

Whidbey is the ideal place for clam digging. Some of the available species are the Manila, Native Littleneck, Butter clams and Horseshoe clams. Scott Fraser, chef at Kasteel Franssen in Oak Harbor, likes to prepare clams in this spicy, low fat manner. He recommends serving them with a chilled Gewurztraminer wine.

2 pounds clams (preferably Butter clams)
1 tablespoon chopped garlic
1 tablespoon chopped ginger
1/4 cup white wine
1/4 cup rice wine vinegar
2 tablespoons black bean sauce
2 tablespoons oyster sauce
red pepper flakes to taste
6 drops sesame seed oil
1 chopped green onion (reserving a bit
    for garnish)
sesame seeds for garnish

Combine all ingredients in a large sauté pan, except for clams and sesame seeds. Bring to boil and cook until it is reduced by a little bit. Add the clams and steam until they open. Garnish with seed and bits of green onion.

Red Potato and Snap Pea Salad

Warm weather fare often includes a potato salad. Invite your friends and family to try this appealing summer favorite that combines garden fresh vegetables, herbs and nuts.

2 pounds red potatoes
2 cups fresh snap peas
1 (14 3/4 ounce) jar marinated
    artichoke hearts, drained
2 tablespoons chopped pecans
1/3 cup snipped parsley
1/3 cup grated Parmesan cheese
Honey Dijon salad dressing
fresh chives for garnish

Cook the potatoes in boiling, salted water for 25 minutes, or until tender. Drain and chill for 30 minutes. Wash and string the peas. Cut the potatoes in large bite size chunks. Halve the peas and artichokes. Place potatoes, peas and artichokes in a large bowl. Add the pecans, parsley, and Parmesan. Toss gently with salad dressing to taste. Top with chives.

Our favorite herb to grow is chives. It is a hearty herb that will grow well outside or inside in a window sill pot. Chives look like tall slender grass and produce a lovely lavender bloom that we like to use as a garnish in soups and salads. The chives have a distinctive, yet light, onion flavor and should always be used without cooking. Simply snip your fresh chives with scissors and enjoy the zest they provide!

Grilled Shrimp

Add this "easy to prepare" dish to your barbecue menu! Serve the salsa as an accompaniment to the shrimp.

1/2 cup unsalted butter
1/2 cup oil
1 tablespoon, each, fresh parsley, thyme and cilantro
4 garlic cloves crushed
1 tablespoon chopped green onion
salt and pepper to taste
1 1/2 pounds medium shrimp in shells
lemon slices for garnish

Combine all ingredients and allow to marinate for 5 hours in the refrigerator. Stir occasionally. Thread shrimp on skewers and grill over medium-hot coals for 2 minutes on each side. Arrange on a platter and garnish with lemon slices.

Pineapple Red Onion Salsa

2 tablespoons fresh cilantro
1 green pepper
1 small red onion
1 1/2 cups fresh pineapple pieces
2 tablespoons white wine vinegar
1/4 teaspoon salt

Use your food processor to mince cilantro for 1 minute before adding pepper and onion. Mince and add pineapple and process again, leaving small diced pieces of pineapple. Put salsa in a bowl and mix in vinegar and salt. Refrigerate and bring to room temperature before serving.

Lemon Basil Capellini

We like to look for recipes that offer versatility and this pasta is certainly one of those. This is the perfect pasta to serve in small portions preceding an entreé. It is also great to make ahead and take to a picnic. Or, you can add heated cream to the pasta for a delightful main dish.

zest of 1 lemon
juice of 1 lemon
1 1/2 tablespoons melted butter
1 1/2 tablespoons extra virgin olive oil
2 tablespoons fresh snipped basil
2 teaspoons fresh snipped parsley
8 ounces cappelini
Parmesan cheese

Use a peeler or citrus zester to remove strips of lemon zest. Put the zest, juice, butter, oil and herbs in a bowl large enough to hold and toss the cooked pasta. Cook the pasta in boiling water, for 2-3 minutes. Drain the noodles and add them to the bowl immediately. Repeatedly lift the noodles to coat with the other ingredients. Serve with grated Parmesan.

When David and Pat Howell moved to Whidbey Island, they brought with them incredible energy and determination focused on the arts. Each summer, Coupeville's town park reverberates with the sounds of music. "Concerts on the Cove" provides a wonderful way to spend an afternoon in a charming seaport town. Pack a picnic lunch, including the Howell's chilled pasta, and head to the park to enjoy the sights and sounds of Whidbey Island.

Captain Whidbey Ginger Steamed Mussels

The Captain Whidbey Inn is a rustic log inn that was built in 1907. Warm hospitality, excellent food, and comfortable lodging are offered to guests. The Inn overlooks Whidbey's picturesque Penn Cove where the sweet mussels are grown and harvested. Captain John Stone has a classic fifty-two foot ketch, "Cutty Sark," which regularly sails Penn Cove and beyond. During the Mussel Festival "Cutty Sark" cruises through the cove to allow guests to watch the mussel farming process.

John Stone, innkeeper of the Captain Whidbey Inn, hosts an annual Mussel Festival. This "tribute to local mollusks" promises great fun and a culinary experience like no other! Mussel cooking techniques are demonstrated, guest chefs prepare elaborate meals, and there is wine tasting too. The festival also includes a Mussel Recipe Contest and a Mussel Chowder Off featuring local restaurants. All of this, in addition to the actual Mussel Eating Contest! Try this specialty of the house.

1 tablespoon chopped ginger
1/2 cup chopped scallions
   (both green and white parts)
2 cloves minced garlic
1 teaspoon black pepper
2 small, hot chili peppers, seeds removed,
   finely diced
1 tablespoon sesame oil
1/4 cup vinegar
2 tablespoons soy sauce
1/2 cup Sake (rice wine)
4 dozen mussels, cleaned and de-bearded

In a large mixing bowl, combine all ingredients except mussels. Add rinsed and dried mussels; cover pan tightly. Cook over medium heat until mussels open; approximately 5 minutes. Discard any that do not open. Remove from heat and swirl in sauce. Serve in individual bowls with ginger sauce.

4 Appetizer Servings

Whidbey's Coffee Cheesecake

This is the most seductive, creamy cheesecake we have ever discovered! We are convinced the success of this cheesecake is due to the fact that chilled Whidbey's coffee is one of the key ingredients.

Graham Cracker Crust

1 1/3 cups graham cracker crumbs
1/3 cup melted margarine
1/4 cup sugar

Preheat oven to 375°. Combine ingredients in a bowl. Press crumbs firmly onto the bottom and 2 inches up the side of a springform pan. Bake for 8 minutes and cool. Set aside.

Cheesecake

4 (8 ounce) packages Neufchatel cheese
1 cup sugar
4 eggs
1/2 cup cold Whidbey's coffee
1 teaspoon vanilla

Preheat oven to 325°. Before you begin the cheesecake, make the coffee very strong and set aside, allowing it to cool. In a large bowl or food processor, beat cheese on high speed until light and fluffy. Beat in sugar. Add eggs, one at a time. Gradually beat in coffee and vanilla. Beat on high for 4-5 minutes. Pour into prepared crust. Bake 1 hour or until center has just set. Turn off the heat and leave the cheesecake in the oven, with the door closed, for 30 minutes longer. Chill completely. Serve with a cup of freshly brewed Whidbey's coffee!

Whidbey's Coffee Company was started in 1989 when Dan Ollis purchased his first espresso cart. He previously sold coffee at fairs, provided catering services, and now offers high quality coffee available in whole or ground beans. "Captain's Choice" is the island favorite with a smooth, slightly spicy taste that makes a unique espresso and an outstanding drip cup of coffee.

Summertime
Raspberry Cake

Prepare this delightful, frozen cake for sudden get-togethers during the last lazy weeks of summer. Experiment with different flavors. For example, you may want to try a mocha yogurt with the raspberry, or substitute strawberries for the raspberries. Be creative with this quick and refreshing palate pleaser!

1 (12 ounce) pound cake
1 cup raspberry preserves
1/4 cup orange juice
2 pints raspberry sorbet, softened
2 pints raspberry-vanilla frozen yogurt, softened
1 (10 ounce) package frozen raspberries in syrup, thawed

Cut cake into 1/4 inch thick slices. Fit the slices tightly into the bottom of a 9 inch springform pan. Cook the preserves and juice in a small saucepan over medium heat, stirring frequently for 14 minutes. It should be reduced to 2/3 cup. Spread half of this mixture over cake in pan. Freeze 15 minutes. Spoon sorbet over cake; smooth top. Arrange more cake slices to cover sorbet. Spread remaining preserve mixture over cake. Freeze 15 minutes. Spoon yogurt over cake; smooth top. Cover and freeze overnight or up to 1 week. Pureé berries in processor. Cover and refrigerate. For serving, release pan sides from cake, slice and ladle pureéd berries over cake slices.

Summer Thirst Quenchers
to enjoy on a balmy Whidbey afternoon.

Sparkling Orange Iced Tea

Freeze a Johnny Jump-up or rose petal in the bottom of your ice cube tray cups to use in your tall tea glasses. Pairing flavored tea with fruit juices is delightfully cool and refreshing.

1 1/3 cups orange tea concentrate (directions below)
1 1/3 cups chilled orange-pineapple juice
1 1/3 cups chilled sparkling water

Over high heat, boil 5 cups water with 12 orange flavored tea bags. Reduce to 4 cups; cover and chill. (Concentrate will keep 2 weeks when refrigerated). For the iced tea, combine the concentrate, juice and water. Use a fresh orange slice as garnish on the glass.

Berry Cooler

1 cup strawberries, rinsed and hulled   juice of 1/2 lemon
1 cup raspberries, rinsed   1 cup sparkling water
1 cup blackberries, rinsed   whole berries for garnish
1 teaspoon sugar

Pureé the strawberries and pour into a large pitcher. Pureé the other berries with sugar and lemon juice. Line a strainer with cheesecloth and pour the berry mixture through the strainer, pushing with the back of a spoon to release juices from the pulp. Add to the strawberry pureé and blend. Pour into frosted glasses. Add ice cubes and sparkling water. Stir, garnish and serve.

Goombay Smash

1 1/4 cups fresh orange juice   1 1/2 cups rum
1 1/4 cups pineapple juice   1/4 cup apricot brandy

Mix all ingredients in a blender for 6 seconds. Pour into ice filled glasses and garnish with orange slices and maraschino cherries.

Index

Tourist Information

Island Transit
360-678-7771

Harbor Airlines
1-800-359-3220

Oak Harbor Chamber of Commerce
360-675-3535

Coupeville Chamber of Commerce
360-678-5434

Freeland Chamber of Commerce
360-331-1980

Langley Chamber of Commerce
360-221-6765

Clinton Chamber of Commerce
360-321-6455

Oak Harbor Marina
360-679-2628

Coupeville Harbormaster
360-678-5020

Langley Marina
360-321-5945

Port of South Whidbey
360-321-5494

Deception Pass State Park
360-675-2417

Ft. Casey State Park
360-678-4519

Ft. Ebey State Park
360-678-4636

South Whidbey State Park
360-331-4559

Seabolt's Smoked Seafood
360-675-6485

Washington State Ferry
1-800-843-3779

Concerts on the Cove
360-678-4684

Whidbey's Greenbank Farm
360-678-7700

Whidbey Island Winery
360-221-4941

Whidbey Island Brew Co.
360-221-8373

Meerkerk Gardens
360-678-1912

Penn Cove Kayak Adventures
360-678-7900

Sassafras Herb Farm
360-678-7135

Mutiny Bay Gourmet
1-800-501-6668

Penn Cove Mussels
360-678-4803

The Captain Whidbey Inn
360-678-4097

North Island B & B
360-675-7080

Maxwelton Manor
360-221-5199

Island Tyme B & B
360-221-5078

Ft. Casey Inn
360-678-8792

Twickenham House B & B
360-221-2334